Friendship
WITH THE
HOLY SPIRIT

The Revival Relationship

JOHN R. VAN GELDEREN
EXPANDED AND UPDATED

REVIVALFOCUS
MINISTRIES

FRIENDSHIP WITH THE HOLY SPIRIT:
The Revival Relationship

Published by Revival Focus
www.RevivalFocus.com

Printed in the United States of America

Scripture quotations are from the Holy Bible, King James
Version.

Italics in Scripture quotations are the emphasis of the author.

Cover Image: Arten/Shutterstock
Graphic Design: Alicia King

ISBN-13 (softcover): 978-0-9906693-0-2
ISBN-10 (softcover): 0990669300

To order copies of this book and other Revival Focus
products in bulk quantities, please contact us at
1-800-656-7896.

DEDICATION

To the memory of Charlie Kittrell
A vibrant example of friendship with the Holy Spirit
to the glory of God

CONTENTS

PREFACE

The reissuing of this book includes minor revisions with two major exceptions. First, I have sought to make clear in the revival accounts in the first and last chapters that *to God alone goes the glory*. Second, I have added a chapter on spiritual guidance (chapter 7).

The purpose of this book is to help readers experience a vibrant relationship with the Holy Spirit by their realizing and responding to who the Holy Spirit is to them. Its focus is purposefully limited to the divine-human relationship. Many outstanding written works provide a fuller theology of the Holy Spirit. In this work I have sought not to take an academic approach and quote a multitude of authors who take the same position I do. However, I provide recommended reading at the back of the book that emphasizes similar truth to what you will find in this book. My burden is simply to let the authority of the Scripture be the authority. May the Spirit of truth give life to all that is in this book that is truly founded on the Word of truth!

John R. Van Gelderen
Manchester, Michigan, June 2014

Chapter One

THE REVIVAL SPIRIT

"We finished at 12:15 a.m. The meeting lasted for nearly two hours in confession, prayer, testimony, and song, again, all led by the prompting of the Spirit. The glory of God was being revealed. Dave said he had never been in prayer meetings like these." So reads an entry in my journal from July 2000. Not only had David O'Gorman, my pastor friend whom I was visiting in Ireland, never before experienced prayer meetings like these, but neither had I. Yet this was the third consecutive night of glorious two-hour after-meetings (which are simply meetings after the meetings!) that finished around midnight—and more were to come.

As we'll soon see, this is an example of what can occur when God's people enter into—in earnest—their friendship with the Holy Spirit. This certainly was a new dimension for me. In fact, I've never been the same since those days. This is true for many others. The lasting impact of such an occurrence is remarkable. The Spirit of revival manifested the presence of God so powerfully that backslidden and mediocre saints were restored to spiritual life—life in the Spirit—and the unsaved received eternal life. This was revival! How did it begin?

David O'Gorman believes that God had been preparing His people for some time. In various ways God had been breaking up fallow ground, much of this occurring among the young people. This preparation was of key significance for the revival that followed.

Let me take you to a scenario in Scotland that took place one week prior to the one I described above. This rendering is taken from the introduction to my book *The Wind of the Spirit*:

> Gray clouds nearly blanketed the sky. A damp, chilly ocean breeze briskly hurried in from the western shoreline approximately one hundred yards away, scampered through the fishing village, and skipped along across the peat bogs to the east. Though the day seemed dreary, my heart thrilled with joy and awesome wonder as I fixed my gaze on the village church in Barvas—a standing reminder of the mighty Spirit of Revival. It was mid-July of 2000. My wife and I were on the Isle of Lewis, located off the northwest coast of Scotland. Just fifty years before this brisk and windy but summer day, the Wind of the Spirit blew across the island. The Lewis Awakening began in December of 1949 in Barvas and continued until 1953 throughout the island. One cannot but think that if God has done it before, and is the unchanging Almighty, He can do it again!
>
> I first became acquainted with the Lewis Revival by reading a brief article about it in the mid-1980s. Immediately my heart was quickened in reading of God's wonderful works. In the

mid-'90s, I listened to an audiotape of Duncan Campbell, whom God used as the primary declarer of truth during the revival. Again God stirred my heart deeply. Since then the Lord brought to me several books written by Duncan Campbell, more audiotapes of his preaching, a video of testimonies from the revival, Duncan Campbell's audio and written account of the awakening, and a biography of Campbell. So my wife and I, in God's gracious leading, took a trip to the Isle of Lewis as a part of a missions trip during the summer of 2000. Here God providentially led us to meet and fellowship with four people who were saved during the revival. The glow of God still shines in their countenances. God taught us much in those precious days.

Yet God had been preparing my heart especially in the eight years previous to this trip. After five years as an assistant to my father, Wayne Van Gelderen, Sr., I entered full-time evangelism in January of 1992. At the same time period, my father asked a group of young preachers to read the two-volume biography of Hudson Taylor, written by Taylor's son and daughter-in-law. God used the pen of Hudson Taylor as he exposited certain Bible passages, along with an inductive study of Galatians and Ephesians, to open my eyes to life-changing truths. I saw the futility of flesh-dependence and the absolute necessity of God-dependence to access Spirit-enablement. Those truths budded and blossomed over the next few years. God cultivated faith in my heart during this rich spiritual pilgrimage.

Then on Christmas Day 1998—I'll never forget it—I began reading a Christmas gift from my wife, the book *By My Spirit* by Jonathan Goforth. Though the noise of Christmas festivities surrounded me, I could not put the book down. The printed preaching of Goforth highlighted overlooked promises in the Word of God. God burned in my heart the possibility of an access by faith for revival blessing. Noting that God used an intensive study on the Holy Spirit to bring Goforth to faith regarding revival, I began a similar study.

The impact has been revolutionary. Along the way, God deepened my understanding of God-dependence for Spirit-enabling. "Christ in you" became utterly real and life-changing. Oh, I have failed—but He has never failed when trusted. The Spirit cultivated, and is cultivating, faith for personal and corporate revival.[1]

This study that I did on the Holy Spirit during the first half of 1999 exploded truth across my heart. So that summer, several of my friends and I met to talk seriously about seeking God's face in revival. We agreed that wherever we were in our various ministries around the country, we would take time to pray daily for the outpouring of the Spirit in revival. Although at times my implementation of this was meager—very meager—it was at least a start. Also, in my ministry of evangelism for local church meetings, I began to preach an entire series of messages on the ministry of the Holy Spirit.

In the summer of 1999, my wife Mary Lynn and I discussed what we might do to celebrate our fifteenth wedding anniversary the next summer. I had been doing a case study of the Lewis revival, and I suggested we go to Scotland to investigate the revival. Seeing that Mary Lynn was genuinely excited about the idea, I suggested that we pray for God to open an opportunity for us to do some ministry in that part of the world. That would help us get over to the British Isles so that we could also go to Lewis. We began to pray that morning. That evening we received an e-mail from David O'Gorman inviting us back to his church in Ireland for a meeting.

Once on Lewis, we attended the mid-week service at the church in Barvas, where the revival had begun. Afterward, the interim pastor, an Irish evangelist who was there for only one month, invited us to the manse for tea and biscuits (in America we would say "to the parsonage for tea and cookies"!).

This evangelist had been trained under Duncan Campbell. His wife's parents had been converted during the Lewis revival. This man had also invited another pastor and his wife, who were there on vacation, to his home that afternoon. Both sets of their parents had been converted during the revival. And an older gentleman who himself had been converted in the revival came. What blessed fellowship we had! We talked much of revival. At times we would stop and sing a hymn. Often, in Scottish style, they would sing a psalm. We also prayed together. Truly it was a blessed time. In fact, later the older gentleman who had visited that day wrote me

a letter saying that the time at the manse reminded him of
times during the revival.

On the way back across the island, Mary Lynn noted to
me that these people were following the Holy Spirit. There
was nothing manipulated or contrived in what they did. They
spontaneously followed the Spirit. The thought impressed
me greatly.

Several days later, we arrived in Dublin, Ireland, where I
preached in the Sunday morning service at David O'Gorman's
church. Then over dinner we enjoyed fellowship with our
good friend David and his wife Valerie. I told them much
of what I've rehearsed in the previous paragraphs. Valerie
wondered out loud where God might take all this.

The next day the church met at a camp in the picturesque
town of Avoca, Ireland, for a week of meetings. Throughout
the week I preached a series on the ministry of the Holy
Spirit, dealing with the Spirit-filled life—the very essence of
the revived life. Monday ended with a "singspiration." I did
not, however, sense the life of God in it. This would not help
the church camp. I prayed that if God wanted me to speak
with David about it, He would open the way for me to do so.
The following morning God answered my prayer as I came
across my pastor friend while I was out on a walk.

When I mentioned to him that I did not sense the life of
God in the singspiration, he agreed. I reminded him of our
time in Lewis and suggested that we depend on the Holy

Spirit to guide our time in the after-meetings to come that week. So after preaching the next morning and then again in the evening—and God's breath was on that service, which focused on Galatians 2:20—David announced that we would meet again after the dessert time but that we were going to do things a little differently. He told those gathered that he would explain at the meeting.

I suppose about thirty or so folks came that night about ten o'clock. We were seated in a circle of chairs. David said, "We're going to do things a little differently tonight. I am turning this meeting over to the Holy Spirit. I know that it may sound a little scary. But let's just depend on the Spirit. If He leads you to sing, start singing, and we'll join in. If He leads you to pray, then pray. If He leads you to testify, then give a testimony. But don't do anything unless the Spirit leads you to do so. Let's depend on Him."

Since the previous night had been a typical singspiration, one might have expected there to be singing. But instead, someone began to pray; after he finished, another began. Within ten minutes we were all aware that God was meeting with His people. There was nothing weird. It was just an awareness of the presence of God. This, of course, makes one aware of his sin. Soon people were confessing their sins. Amazingly, neither Dave nor I had mentioned confession— not that it would have been improper to do so, but we hadn't. Oh, what brokenness before the Lord! Nothing inappropriate was said, but there was a proper transparency before God and men. About a third of the way through the meeting, the group broke out into glorious singing as people had now come clean with God. Oh, the joy of a cleansed conscience and a clean heart! The last third of the meeting was spent praying again. This time it was an intense praying for God to spread His work and to save the lost. The meeting lasted for two hours and seemed like fifteen minutes.

I should mention there were two people in that meeting who got saved that night. One was a young, outgoing girl who said to her parents after the meeting, "I'm afraid. These people know God, and I don't." Her parents then led her to trust in Christ as her Savior. The other was a deaf teenage boy who, although he couldn't hear the prayers, sensed the presence of God. He nudged someone next to him. When they went out, he communicated that he felt as if his chest were going to burst and that he wanted to get saved. The manifest presence of God is a universal language.

God met with us night after night. The services were filled with blessing, and the after-meetings were glory meetings. This was a sustained moving of God beyond just one night. Many were changed. And the impact has continued. Young people who were once worldly after these meetings attended Bible college to prepare for the ministry. The church has grown significantly and seen far more people saved since this time than ever before.

I must hasten to add that when we had been on the Isle of Lewis, God had allowed us to spend some time with a man who as a young person had been converted during the Lewis awakening fifty years earlier. Growing quickly, he had become an intercessor and joined the praying men of Barvas as the revival progressed. On at least two occasions, the fire had fallen when this young man had prayed with the other men. This man had met with my wife and me in the very building in which he had been converted. At the conclusion of our two hours together, he had prayed for us in a very special way. I believe that the blessing in Ireland that followed the very next week was directly linked to this intercessor's prayer. Also, I later discovered that a prayer warrior in the United States who prayed regularly for our ministry had specifically interceded for us during that time as well and had felt confident of God's blessing in our time in Ireland even before I testified to him of the details of God's revival working. I was not the intercessor—I simply had the privilege of witnessing firsthand God's blessing.

What I saw in those meetings in Ireland demonstrated in a deep way the living reality of friendship with the Spirit—and its blessed effects. Of course, what my wife and I observed was a corporate setting. Yet the individual impact on me and on many others in those meetings has been forever life changing, because the same dynamic that transforms groups also transforms individual lives.

A classic testimony of personal revival comes from the life of Walter Wilson, a preacher, part-time medical doctor, and fervent soul-winner who founded a church and a Bible college in Kansas City. He relates the following in his book on the Holy Spirit entitled *Ye Know Him*:

> The first seventeen years of my life after meeting the Saviour were years of much Bible study, much activity, and no fruit. I had been taught that it was wrong to expect any fruit. Teachers had also instructed me to not speak to the Holy Spirit in prayer nor commune with Him about the work of God but to go to the Father with every matter. The barrenness of my ministry and the lack of results in my service was the cause of no little sorrow and regret.
>
> One day the Lord graciously sent across my path a man of God who said to me, "What is the Holy Spirit to you?" I replied that He was one of the persons of the Godhead. The servant of God answered that this was a true statement but did not answer his question, "What is the Holy Spirit *to* you? What does He mean *to* you?" This inquiry produced a deep heart searching and I replied, "He is nothing to me at all. I know who He is, but I have no personal relationship with Him." My friend assured me that my life was barren and my ministry fruitless because of this neglect. I had been treating the Holy Spirit as a servant of mine. I would ask Him to come help me when I would teach a class. To be more explicit, I really asked the Father to send His Spirit to help me. This left the Spirit as a servant subject to my call and request. He was never more than an agent of the

Godhead to serve me whenever I felt His need and asked the Father for His ministry.

The message which this Christian brought to my heart roused within me a great desire to know the Spirit and to serve Him successfully. I had a fear, however, of doing the wrong thing and felt that perhaps the Father and Lord Jesus would be offended if I should go directly to the Spirit about any matter. About this time . . .[2]

We will finish this story later. But what about you? What is the Holy Spirit *to you*? What does He mean *to you*? In other words, how is your relationship with the Holy Spirit? Do you have a vibrant, genuine relationship with Him? Would you say that you have a *friendship with the Holy Spirit*?

The primary Scripture text for the basis of our study throughout this book is the benediction found in 2 Corinthians 13:14: "The grace of the Lord Jesus Christ, and the love of God, and *the communion of the Holy Ghost, be with you all*. Amen." The key word of this text, "communion," means "partnership, fellowship, sharing together, companionship, joint participation, or functioning together as one." What a picturesque term! What a term of friendship! The inspired prayer of the apostle reveals a burden for *all* to know this *communion*. This, by way of application, includes every believer.

Since we as believers are to commune with the Holy Spirit, we must develop a friendship with our heavenly partner. Yet how can a believer, the human partner, develop a biblically balanced, vibrant relationship with the Holy Spirit, the heavenly partner? Foundationally, in order to fulfill our responsibility in this miraculous friendship, we must understand who our heavenly partner really is *to us*. This will provide insight into our relational responsibilities *to Him*. So from the vast realm of scriptural truth regarding the Holy Spirit, we are going to focus for the next four chapters on four biblical affirmations of who He is to us.

In the following two chapters, we'll build on that foundation with some key issues, and in the final chapter, we'll draw some conclusions. As you read this book, it is my prayer that you will come to experience a vibrant friendship with the Holy Spirit by realizing and responding to who the Holy Spirit is to you.

Questions for Personal Reflection

1. How many prayer meetings have you attended in which two hours seemed like fifteen minutes because the Holy Spirit was in charge?

2. In what ways can you relate to Walter Wilson's testimony of largely fruitless ministry?

3. Do you desire a vibrant friendship with the Holy Spirit? If so, why not ask God right now to bring you into this kind of relationship?

Chapter Two

THE DIVINE PARTNER

One of the stirring chapters of revival history is the Korean revival of 1907. In Jonathan Goforth's account of this mighty revival, he emphasizes that the Korean saints honored the Holy Spirit. When they began to honor the Spirit, they stopped quenching the Spirit of revival, and revival fires swept Korea. According to Jonathan's wife Rosalind, her husband's sermon "When the Spirit's Fire Swept Korea," which preaches the story, was his most blessed message.[1]

Our text, 2 Corinthians 13:14, delineates the Godhead by referring to "the grace of the Lord Jesus Christ, and the love of God [the Father], and the communion of the Holy Ghost." Since the Holy Spirit is the divine partner with whom we seek to develop relationship, we must honor the Spirit as God just as we honor the Father and the Son. Let's ask some questions to guide us through this chapter.

Is the Holy Spirit Truly God?

This question seems almost unnecessary. Undoubtedly many would answer yes. Yet for many, saying that the Holy Spirit is God is merely a doctrinal affirmation rather than a practical reality. The Holy Spirit is not really given the status of deity in the practice of many in their daily lives.

He is viewed more as a second-class citizen in the Godhead. Therefore, in all practicality, these people are not true Trinitarians, because although they acknowledge the Spirit as God in their doctrine, they do not treat Him as God in their practice.

However, in Matthew 28:19 Jesus commands us to make disciples and to baptize them in the name [singular] of the Father and of the Son and of the Holy Spirit. The Spirit is thus given the status of the Godhead. In Psalm 139 we see that He is omnipresent. And only God is omnipresent. The Spirit is called "the eternal Spirit" in Hebrews 9:14. Only God is eternal. The Spirit is deity—He is God.

Should the Holy Spirit Be Glorified as God?

Should the Holy Spirit be glorified as God along with the Father and the Son? In remembering our first question "Is the Holy Spirit truly God?" the answer ought to be obvious. When the Scripture says, "Honor God" but does not specify which person of the Godhead it is referring to, does it not include all three? Yet a preacher once came to me quite exercised and exclaimed, "You can't glorify the Spirit!" But where does it say that in the Bible? If we cannot glorify the Spirit, He is less than God, and we no longer have a true Trinity.

Some object, asserting, "You're placing too much emphasis on the Holy Spirit." But how can we place too much emphasis on God? This reveals the real problem:for some the Holy Spirit is less than God. Would anyone say, "You're placing too much emphasis on the Father," or, "You're placing too much emphasis on Jesus Christ"? Why does the Holy Spirit not receive the honor due to One who is a part of the Godhead? Now if we were to uplift one person of the Godhead to the exclusion of the other two, that would be false doctrine. But that is not the issue here. This is not a matter of deemphasizing the Father or the Son; it is a matter of recognizing that we must not neglect the Holy Spirit. It is a matter of getting back into balance.

Some object by citing what Jesus said when referring to the Spirit, "He shall glorify me" (John 16:14). While this is most certainly true, Jesus never said that we are not to honor the Spirit. Some take a leap at this point that jumps beyond what Jesus actually said. They conclude that we *cannot* glorify the Spirit. But scripturally there is a sense in which each person of the Godhead glorifies the other two. As A. W. Tozer points out, the persons of the Godhead are not jealous of each other!

Others object by quoting what Jesus said of the Spirit: "He shall not speak of himself" (John 16:13). They argue from this that we are not to talk about the Holy Spirit. Ironically, this verse is in a three-chapter-long sermon about the Holy Spirit preached by Christ Himself. Notice as well that Jesus did not say, "He shall not speak *about* Himself" but *"of* Himself." The term translated *of* literally means "from." The

Spirit does not speak *from* Himself apart from the Father and the Son. The Godhead always works in perfect unison. But the truth is that the Holy Spirit does speak *about* Himself. How else could we know about the Spirit except through the inspired Word that "came not in old time by the will of man: but holy men of God spake as they were moved by the Holy Ghost" (2 Pet. 1:21)?

The Scripture contains 347 explicit references to the Holy Spirit: there are 86 in the Old Testament and 261 in the New Testament. In light of the relative brevity of the New Testament, is this not a considerable number? And this does not even include words like "grace" in which the Spirit is implicitly mentioned. This in no way diminishes the far greater number of references to Christ in keeping with the Spirit's role to testify of the Son (see John 15:26), but it does show that it is legitimate to talk about the Holy Spirit.

Also, if we interpret the phrase "He shall not speak of Himself" to mean "*about* Himself," then in order to be consistent we would have to interpret the phrase in John 14:10, in which Jesus said "I speak not of myself," the same way. If the former phrase means we are not to talk about the Spirit, then the latter phrase would mean that we are not to speak about Jesus—which of course would be folly.

The Scripture states, "Now the Lord is that Spirit" (2 Cor. 3:17). The inspired Word of God teaches the lordship of the Spirit. The Holy Spirit is coequal with the Father and the

Son and may rightly be glorified as such. Since He is Lord, He should be honored as Lord. The Nicene Creed, written over sixteen hundred years ago, says, "I believe in the Holy Ghost, the Lord and Giver of life, which proceedeth from the Father and the Son, and with the Father and the Son together is worshiped and glorified." The Athanasian Creed, written over fifteen hundred years ago, states, "Such as the Father is, such is the Son, and such is the Holy Ghost." Remember the oneness of God. Although there are three persons in the Godhead, there is only one God. Therefore, in honoring God we may rightly honor each person of the Godhead. The Doxology articulates the truth so well:

> Praise God, from whom all blessings flow;
> Praise Him, all creatures here below;
> Praise Him above, ye heav'nly host;
> Praise Father, Son, and Holy Ghost!

Who Reveals Christ?

Who reveals the Father? The Son, for Jesus said, "He that hath seen me hath seen the Father" (John 14:9). And who reveals the Son? The Spirit, for Jesus said, "He shall glorify me: for he shall receive of mine, and shall shew it unto you" (John 16:14). The Spirit shows us Christ. He reveals the Son. As the Son reveals the Father, so the Spirit reveals the Son. Why is this important?

Jesus said, "All men should honour the Son, even as they honour the Father" (John 5:23). Why? Since the Son is the express revelation of the Father, He must be honored as the Father is honored. Jesus continued, "He that honoureth not the Son honoureth not the Father which hath sent him." Again, why? Since the Son reveals the Father, if we do not honor the Son, we cannot truly honor the Father. Therefore, when the Jehovah's Witnesses, for example, claim to honor the Father yet deny the deity of Christ, they are deceived. Since the Son reveals the Father, in order to honor the Father, we must honor the Son.

In light of this principle, if we desire to honor the Son, whom must we honor? The Spirit, for the Spirit reveals the Son who sent Him. Do you see the point? The Spirit is our only access to seeing Jesus! The Spirit shows us Christ (see John 16:14). If we do not honor the Spirit and thus rightly relate to the Spirit, then we block our avenue of seeing Jesus. So if we have a passion for the Lord Jesus Christ, if we desire that Christ be exalted in our sight, if we long to know Him and the power of His resurrection, then we must properly relate to the Holy Spirit, for the Spirit is the One who will glorify Christ and reveal Christ to us.

Near the end of a week-long meeting at which I preached on the ministry of the Holy Spirit, members of a local church sang "Victory in Jesus." The pastor later commented to me that his people sang the song on a new level. He noted that although the preaching had dealt with the truths of the Spirit, the effect was the exaltation of Christ. Should we be surprised?

What Is the Spirit Like?

The Spirit is like Jesus, for He is called "the Spirit of Jesus Christ" (Phil. 1:19). When Philip requested of Jesus, "Lord, show us the Father, and it sufficeth [is sufficient for] us," Jesus responded with that heart-searching question, "Have I been so long time with you, and yet hast thou not known Me?" Then He declared, "He that hath seen me hath seen the Father" (John 14:8–9). Perhaps the Spirit responds to us in similar tones, "Have I been so long time with you, and yet you have not known me? He that has known me has known the Son."

Jesus said, "He that believeth on me, believeth not on me, but on him that sent me. And he that seeth me seeth him that sent me" (John 12:44–45). The principle shown here implies that he who believes in the Holy Spirit believes not in the Holy Spirit but in Christ who sent Him. And he who sees (spiritually) the Holy Spirit sees (spiritually) Christ who sent Him. This is the way we see Jesus today. In fact, in John 14:16–18 Jesus told His disciples that He would be sending the Spirit. Although the world did not know the Spirit, Jesus emphasized to His disciples, "Ye know him; for he dwelleth with you, and shall be in you." Then Jesus restated the same truth in a different way: "I will not leave you comfortless: *I* will come to you." Therefore, it is not just a matter of the Spirit coming in Christ's stead but the Spirit bringing Christ to us. If we long to know Christ intimately, we must get to know the Spirit. As we do, we will surely exclaim, "What a friend we have in Jesus!"

On a personal note, there was a time in my life when although I was saved, I did not sense a close relationship with the Lord Jesus. This bothered me and at the same time puzzled me. However, since the days when the Lord stirred me to develop a right relationship with the Holy Spirit, the Son has risen gloriously in my view. Now seeing Jesus is everything to me! The more we relate to the Spirit of Jesus, the more the Son of Righteousness rises in our view and will rise until we see Him in His full-orbed glory.

When the Third Great Awakening commenced in America, Spurgeon preached to his people:

> It is the work of the Holy Spirit that I wish to especially direct to your attention, and may I as well mention the reason why I do. It is this: in the United States of America there has been a great awakening [1858]. Two hundred and fifty thousand people profess to have been regenerated. . . . Now this great work in America has been manifestly caused by the outpouring of the Spirit. . . . To have a similar effect produced in this land, the one thing we must seek is the outpouring of the Holy Spirit. I thought that perhaps my writing

about the work of the Holy Spirit might fulfill the text, "Them that honor me I will honor" (1 Samuel 2:30). My sincere desire is to honor the Holy Spirit, and if He will be pleased to honor His church in return, unto Him be the glory forever.[2]

The Third Great Awakening did spread across the sea to England and beyond. Since the Holy Spirit is the divine partner, we must honor the Spirit as God. This must be true not only in our doctrine but in our practice. May the Spirit then be pleased by granting His reviving presence!

Questions for Personal Reflection

1. Do you honor the Holy Spirit as God along with the Father and the Son—not just in doctrine but in practice? Or is the Spirit somewhat neglected in your life? If this has been the case, will you make this right with Him?
2. Have you felt a lack of closeness in your relationship with Jesus?
3. How can a right relationship with the Spirit enhance your relationship with Jesus?

Chapter Three

A PERSONAL PARTNER

On the other end of the phone line, I heard an excited voice exclaim, "John, I had to call and let you know what God did!" It was Sunday. A pastor friend of mine, in whose church I had preached the previous week on the ministry of the Spirit, was calling. Though he had not had a resisting spirit to the message I had given, he admitted to grappling with what he had heard (especially the truth that this chapter presents). Yet this morning in his church, he had preached from Acts 1–2. At the conclusion of the message, he confessed to his congregation that he had neglected the Holy Spirit. He told his people that he was going to be the first to kneel in prayer at the end of the service. Then he asked others to whom God had spoken to join him. Although when I had been there the week before, public response had been minimal, about thirty people joined him this week! In the months following, that church saw remarkable blessings from the Lord.

The text we've been studying, 2 Corinthians 13:14, says, "The communion of the Holy Ghost, be with you all." We noted earlier that the word *communion* [*koinonia*] means "partnership, fellowship, sharing together, companionship, joint participation, functioning together as one." It is a beautiful term of interactive friendship. The definite article "the" before the name "Holy Spirit" grammatically emphasizes the Spirit's person. Since the Holy Spirit is a personal partner, we must treat the Spirit as a person. Consider two key thoughts.

The Holy Spirit Is a Personality

The Spirit of God is not an inanimate object. Yet how often do people look to Him as some kind of spiritual signpost to point the way? But the Spirit is not a signpost or a commodity; He is a person.

The Spirit of God is not an impersonal force. Yet how often do Christians say, "Something told me . . ." But the Spirit is not a something; He is *Someone*. Sadly, for many He is nothing more than an impersonal force. Often this is evidenced when people refer to the Spirit as "it." In conversations with believers, I have heard this often. How would we like to be referred to as an "it"? Perhaps it is time for many to get right with the Holy Spirit in this regard.

Throughout the Upper Room discourse (see John 14–16), the Lord Jesus refers to the Holy Spirit repeatedly as "Him" and "He." Do you get the biblical picture? If we are truly born of the Spirit, then *He,* not "it," lives in us. He is our personal partner. The Spirit-filled life accesses a life—a person—who lives in us to live through us.

The Spirit loves and therefore can be grieved. The Scripture says, "Grieve not the holy Spirit of God, whereby ye are sealed unto the day of redemption" (Eph. 4:30). Mere forces, ideas, or influences cannot love or be grieved. The Spirit stirs the heart and therefore can be quenched. The Scripture says, "Quench not the Spirit" (1 Thess. 5:19). The Spirit teaches, convinces, and leads and therefore can be resisted. May we not be like those Stephen chided, "Ye do always resist the Holy Ghost" (Acts 7:51).

Do you treat the Holy Spirit as a person? Personality must be cultivated. We may be introduced to someone, and therefore we know his or her name. But do we really know that person? Obviously, it takes interaction to cultivate someone's personality. Even so, everyone who is born of the Spirit has been introduced to the Spirit. But it takes interaction to cultivate personality. It takes heartfelt interaction to cultivate friendship. This leads us to our second key thought.

A Friendship Is a Relationship

What makes a good relationship? Communication, appreciation, devotion, and loyalty quickly come to mind. Are not these relational concepts crucial to relating? Again I refer to our text: "communion" means "fellowship, sharing together, and joint participation." In fact, the same word is translated "fellowship" in the phrase "fellowship of the Spirit" (Phil. 2:1). The very term demands an interactive relationship. Communion must be mutual or it is not communion.

Open Communication

Foundational to any healthy relationship is open communication. Since this is the case and yet a most confused point in many people's minds, we will attempt to be thorough on this truth.

Does the Holy Spirit communicate with us? The Scripture says explicitly, "The Spirit . . . beareth witness with our spirit" (Rom. 8:16). Notice with what He bears witness: *our spirit.* He speaks to our inner man, not our outer man. Understanding this can help protect against counterfeits, which we'll address more fully in chapter 7. But the Holy Spirit does communicate to individual believers.

Is this communication to be only a one-way communication, or should we communicate with the Holy Spirit? Well, is the Spirit God? Is He a person? Then the answers ought to be obvious. Sadly, for many this is not the case, and therefore they do not treat the Holy Spirit as a person. They may acknowledge intellectually the personhood of the Spirit, but in practice they really do not depend on this reality. They overlook the practical ramifications of "the Holy Ghost which is in you" (1 Cor. 6:19).

A friend of mine once heard Walter Wilson state the matter with so much common sense: "Personal presence automatically carries with it privileges of conversation." We do not have to get permission to talk to a person. If we cannot communicate with the Holy Spirit, then what is the

Holy Spirit to us but a mere force or a mysterious power or an inanimate object?

What kind of marriage would a couple have if only one partner did all the talking? Setting all fun aside, this kind of marriage partnership would be unhealthy and weak. To have a good relationship, each partner must relate. Two-way communication is necessary for a strong, healthy relationship.

Yet does the Bible teach us to communicate with the Holy Spirit? The answer is yes—both explicitly and implicitly. On the explicit level, our text, an inspired benediction says, "The communion of the Holy Ghost, be with you all." Clearly it is God's will for each believer to commune with the Spirit. To actually "commune," to "fellowship," to "share together," and to "function together as one" inherently demands two-way communication. Communication must be mutual, or it is not communion. If words have meaning and language has integrity, then in order for *the communion of the Holy Spirit* to *be with* us as individuals, we must join in this relationship of God with men. Isn't it absolutely amazing that God desires companionship with us? What a great salvation!

On the implicit level, in the longest treatise on the Holy Spirit given by Christ Himself in John 14–16, Christ says, "I will pray the Father, and he shall give you another Comforter . . . even the Spirit of truth" (John 14:16–17). The word "another" means "another of the same kind." Then Jesus says in the next verse, "I will not leave you comfortless: *I* will come to you" (John 14:18). The Spirit brings Christ to us. To despise or slight the Spirit is to despise or slight "Christ in you."

Another of the same kind has come to stand in Christ's stead and yet to bring Christ to us. Did not the disciples interact with Jesus as a person? Did they not communicate with Him? Since the Spirit is another of the same kind, should we not interact with the Spirit today as the disciples of old did with Christ?

The issue is communication, not necessarily praying. In a marriage relationship, when a husband and wife communicate with each other, they are not praying to each other (unless perhaps the wife is asking for the wallet!). The issue is interaction through communication.

However, is it improper to *ever* (I did not say *only*) address the Holy Spirit in prayer? Is He God? Is He a person? Then again the answers should be obvious. Many get hung up here, and in the name of honoring Jesus or the Father, they dishonor the Spirit of Jesus and the Spirit of the Father. Is this not a contradiction? Let's take just a moment to clear up some of the confusion.

In Ezekiel 37 God commanded the prophet Ezekiel to pray *to* the Holy Spirit: "Come from the four winds, O breath, and breathe upon these slain, that they may live" (Ezek. 37:9). God defines the breath as "my spirit" (Ezek. 37:14). This prayer was to the Spirit of God. This example should settle any questions about the legitimacy of at least some prayer being made to the Spirit.

I suppose the greatest objection to ever directly addressing the Spirit comes from a misunderstanding of what we call the Lord's Prayer. The Lord Jesus said, "After this manner therefore pray ye: Our Father . . ." (Matt. 6:9). Some conclude from this that we are to address only the Father, but this conclusion is problematic in several ways. First, if this means that we can address only the Father, then to be consistent we could not ever address the Son. Do not many people get saved by asking Jesus to save them? Second, if we are to take from this that we can only say "our Father" when we pray, then to be consistent we could only pray the exact words of the Lord's Prayer. This of course would be the vain repetitions of the Roman Catholic "Our Fathers." Third, to take from this that we can only say "our Father" is to miss Christ's opening concept, which we see in His words "After this manner therefore pray ye." The issue here is *manner*, not vain repetition.

The fact is, many people at the time of Christ did pray to Jesus (not the Father) to have mercy on them. As he began to sink, Peter prayed directly to Jesus, "Lord, save me" (Matt. 14:30). The lepers cried out, "Jesus, Master, have mercy on us" (Luke 17:13). Interestingly, there is no Old Testament teaching to support this. People at the time of Christ's incarnation had only the Old Testament. Yet even though praying to Jesus was not taught in the Old Testament, many at the time of Christ prayed directly to Him, as we have just noted. Not to have prayed to the *present* Jesus would have revealed a low view of who He is.

Likewise, though there is little in the New Testament regarding praying to the Spirit, not to pray to the *present* Holy Spirit is to reveal a low view of who He is. Should not we who live in the age of the Spirit cry out to the Spirit as our Helper in time of need? Some object, saying that people cried out to Christ because He was personally standing there with them. But is not that the whole point? The Holy Spirit is just as personally present as Christ was in New Testament times, not only with us but in us. Not to apprehend this truth is to miss the blessing of the indwelling Christ.

The book of Acts records thirteen prayers. Twelve are addressed to "Lord" as opposed to "our Father." Some contexts infer Christ, and in one instance Christ is expressly named. The truth is that the title "Lord" encompasses all three persons of the Godhead and can be used specifically with any one person, including the Holy Spirit. The Scripture declares, "The Lord is that Spirit" (2 Cor. 3:17). Paul under inspiration said, "The Lord direct your hearts into the love of God, and into the patient waiting for Christ" (2 Thess. 3:5). The implication is "May the Lord . . . ," which is essentially a prayer. Since the Father and the Son are named in the last two phrases, the implication is that "the Lord" in the first phrase to whom Paul prayed refers to the Spirit.

Jesus said, "Pray ye therefore the Lord of the harvest, that he will send forth labourers into his harvest" (Matt. 9:38). Who is the Lord of the harvest? The context definitely leans toward the idea that Christ is here referring to someone other than His own person. Who descended in mighty power on the day of Pentecost so that three thousand people were harvested? We are explicitly told that this was the Spirit (see Acts 2). Who told Philip to "go near, and join [himself] to this chariot" so that the Ethiopian eunuch was harvested? We are explicitly told that this was the Spirit (Acts 8:29). Who said to Peter, "Go with them, doubting nothing" so that Cornelius and his household were harvested, thus opening the way to the Gentile harvest? We are explicitly told that this was the Spirit (Acts 10:19–20). Who said to the church at Antioch, "Separate me Barnabas and Saul for the work whereunto I have called them," which led to the first missionary journey of multiple harvests? We are explicitly told that this was the Spirit (Acts 13:2). Who forbade Paul to minister in Asia and Bithynia in order to get them into the Macedonian harvest? We are explicitly told that this was the Spirit (see Acts 16:6–7). So who is the Lord of the harvest? The book of Acts certainly implies that the Lord of the harvest is the Holy Spirit. And Jesus told us, "*Pray* ye therefore the Lord of the harvest, that He will send forth laborers into His harvest."

The hymn writers of the past reflect a proper understanding of appropriate times to address the Spirit in prayer. For example, "Spirit of God, Descend upon My Heart," "Breathe on Me Breath of God," "Spirit of the Living God, Fall Fresh on Me," and "Holy Ghost, with Light Divine." Charles Wesley wrote "Come, Holy Ghost, our Hearts Inspire," "Come, Thou Everlasting Spirit," and "Spirit of Faith, Come Down." Isaac Watts wrote, "Eternal Spirit! Praise We Bring." All these examples directly address the Holy Spirit in prayer. Were all these hymn writers misled? Are congregations sinning every time they sing one of these prayers? Obviously former generations had a better understanding of this issue than the present generation does.

This is not at all to diminish the Father. He is "our Father," and much of the time, if not most of the time, we most certainly will beseech Him as such. In fact, the Spirit enables us to do so. "Ye have received the Spirit of adoption, whereby we cry, Abba, Father" (Rom. 8:15). Also, this in no way should imply a minimizing of the Son. Oh, "that in all things he might have the pre-eminence" (Col. 1:18)! This is to say that where applicable, we must stop slighting the blessed Holy Spirit, who is both the Spirit of the Father and the Spirit of the Son. This is not a matter of getting out of balance but rather of getting back into balance.

All three persons of the Godhead are often mentioned regarding a specific matter in Scripture, but one is emphasized as the prominent person in that particular matter. This both reveals the oneness of God and yet the distinctiveness of each person. When the Spirit is emphasized regarding a matter, we may properly address Him about that matter. The Holy Spirit is the Comforter. How can He truly be the Comforter if we cannot bare to Him our tale of woe? As the *Paraclete,* He is the Helper. Should we not cry out to Him for help in time of need? He is the Lord of the harvest. Should we not talk to Him about guidance and enablement regarding our partnership with Him in the harvest? He is the great Teacher. Should we not ask the author of the inspired Word for illumination of the sacred page? This is the cry of the psalmist: "Open thou mine eyes, that I may behold wondrous things out of thy law" (Ps. 119:18). When the Spirit is the direct agent involved in a matter, then He may be addressed in our praying just as we would address the Father or the Son in matters that relate directly to either the Father or the Son. Quite frankly, as we go throughout the day and cry out "Lord, give me wisdom," who are we talking to?

Once when I was in Ireland, a man asked me, "Can we just say 'Lord' and let God address it to the appropriate person?" I love the simplicity of this question. There is a sense in which addressing any one person of the Godhead is addressing all three, since we are dealing with one God. The problem comes when people willfully neglect the Holy Spirit.

Again, however, the real issue is not prayer as such but rather communication. The Holy Spirit is a person and must be treated as a person. Suppose you are visiting a museum that specializes in ancient artifacts. Suppose three others are making the visit with you, but one of them is appointed as your personal guide. Would it be right to speak only to the other two tourists and never to your personal guide, who is in regular communication with you? Yet is this not what many do to the Spirit?

Jesus said, "It is expedient for you [to your advantage] that I go away: for if I go not away, the Comforter will not come unto you; but if I depart, I will send him unto you" (John 16:7). What a statement! Jesus said it is more advantageous for us if He departs so that His Spirit could come and be our personal companion. For us to ignore this personal relationship with the Spirit is to despise our Savior's throne gift: the gift of the Spirit that He sent from His throne on the Day of Pentecost.

An evangelist friend of mine, years ago, heard Walter Wilson preach. Wilson began by asking those in the audience how many of them had spoken to the Holy Spirit that day. There was little response. Then he told the people that since the Holy Spirit is a person who lives in us, He is always with us, and to have a person always with us and yet never speak to Him is not very nice! This little anecdote certainly helps put the issue into perspective. As a preacher I knew once said, "When you know the family, you can speak to all the family members!"

In light of the overreaction in our day to strange fire, I recognize that many perhaps have never thought much about interaction with the Holy Spirit and are not willfully neglecting Him. This is one matter. It is entirely another matter to willfully neglect interacting with the Holy Spirit as a person. When this is the case, it reveals on the part of the one involved a lack of honoring the Spirit as truly God and a lack of treating the Spirit as truly a person. This reveals a lack of understanding of the genuine Spirit-filled life of Galatians 2:20: "I live; yet not I, but Christ liveth in me." When this is the case, it keeps God's people from accessing the victory of Christ for holiness and service.

Beside open communication, what are some other ways to relate to the Holy Spirit?

Expressed Appreciation

When someone does something for us, courtesy demands that we say thank-you. How often do we ignore the Spirit on this score? While we may rightly thank the Father and the Son, do we forget to thank the Spirit? When our relationship with the Spirit is healthy, gratitude will flow toward the Spirit for all His guidance, comfort, and aid. After discovering some arresting truth in Scripture, how often do we say, "*I* found a wonderful truth in the Word." Is this not arrogantly slighting the Spirit? Is not the reality that the Spirit of truth guided us into truth? When the partnership between us and the Spirit is properly developed, we can say as the early Christians did, "It seemed good to the Holy Ghost, and to us" (Acts 15:28). This inspired example expresses appreciation.

Loyal Devotion

Another key to developing a good relationship is loyal devotion. The Spirit is certainly a loyal and devoted partner in His relationship with us. As the Spirit of Christ, He never leaves us nor forsakes us (see Heb. 13:5–6). (The next chapter will unfold *our* responsibility of loyal devotion to our heavenly partner.)

Since the Holy Spirit is a personal partner, we must treat Him as a person. One lady, after apprehending this truth, said to me, "It was so good to talk with the Holy Spirit!" This makes our walk with God personal and real. Just as salvation is not a religion but a relationship with Jesus Christ, so the Spirit-filled life is not a religion but a relationship with the Holy Spirit.

I remember well when revival swept through a small group of praying believers in the Philippines. An evangelist friend of mine and I were in the midst of a conference there on the Spirit-filled life. As the Spirit of judgment came in power among us, sin was earnestly confessed by those in attendance. Soon wearied believers exchanged spiritual dullness for spiritual joy. As a result of clean hearts and filled lives, God gave a harvest of souls over the next weeks and months that this generation had not seen before in their church. If God has spoken to you about neglecting the Holy Spirit, may your response be as one Filipino pastor prayed, "O Holy Spirit, forgive me for not treating You as a person!"

Questions for Personal Reflection

1. In what ways has the Holy Spirit communicated with you recently?

2. Do you communicate with the Holy Spirit? If not, will you make this right even now?

3. What has the Holy Spirit done for you for which you should thank Him?

Chapter Four

THE SENIOR PARTNER

Years ago, James A. Stewart, an evangelist from Scotland, was preaching in the Orkney Islands in the north of the country. Feeling impressed of the Lord to spend some time alone with God, he did so by walking a cold beach in the early morning hours. He knew that God had brought him out to the seashore for a purpose. As he walked, he became convinced by the Spirit to go Riga in Latvia. He closed the Orkney Island meetings, and within days arrived unannounced and unknown in the Eastern European city of Riga.

When a certain pastor invited him to preach, God sent revival blessing on the congregation. For months Stewart preached throughout many Eastern European countries. Saints were revived, and literally thousands were saved as God poured out His Spirit.[1] Truly Stewart was in partnership with the Spirit, and he knew it. He knew the Spirit's voice. He discerned the difference between the counterfeit guidance of impulse or the enemy and the sure convincement of the Spirit. This and other similar accounts are given in both his autobiography, *I Must Tell*, and his biography, *James Stewart: Missionary*.[2] Oh, how we need to learn to recognize and obey the Holy Spirit!

Our text, 2 Corinthians 13:14, implores, may "the communion of the Holy Ghost, be with you all." Clearly the Holy Spirit, as the heavenly partner in our relationship with Him, is the senior partner. Since the Holy Spirit is the senior partner, we must yield to the Spirit as Lord.

"Now the Lord is that Spirit" (2 Cor. 3:17). The Spirit is called Lord. The Spirit is Lord because the Holy Spirit is the Spirit of Christ, and Christ is the head of the church. When Paul prayed, "The Lord direct your hearts into the love of God, and into the patient waiting for Christ" (2 Thess. 3:5), he calls the Spirit Lord. The lordship of Christ is executed through the lordship of the Spirit.

Since the Spirit is Lord, we must surrender to His lordship. We must yield our will to the will of another. This is not passivity. Passivity would be giving up our will and stopping short at that. However, a passive will is the devil's playground. Surrender to the Spirit means giving up our will and taking on His will. It is exchanging our will for the Spirit's will. It is us willing (an act of choice) to choose the Spirit's will. It is not the Spirit instead of us but us cooperating with the Spirit. It is not idle passivity but active cooperation. This is true surrender.

"Now the Lord is that Spirit: and where the Spirit of the Lord is, there is liberty" (2 Cor. 3:17). We must not only recognize that the Spirit is Lord but also yield to Him as Lord. The second phrase implies "where the Spirit is Lord" or, more clearly, "where the Spirit is yielded to as Lord." This implies dependence on the Spirit's leadership. Our will must be brought into union with the Spirit's will. When this genuinely takes place, there is freedom. Where does this begin?

Directional Surrender

Partnership with the Holy Spirit begins with a directional surrender—a surrender to His direction for our life. The Scripture urges, "I beseech you therefore, brethren . . . that ye present your bodies . . . unto God" (Rom. 12:1). Since the Holy Spirit is the person of the Godhead who indwells the believer, why does Romans 12:1 urge believers to present their bodies to the Spirit of God when the Scripture also states, "Your body is the temple of Holy Ghost which is in you" (1 Cor. 6:19)? Because when we got saved, the Spirit specifically moved into our spirit. Applying Romans 12:1 presents the body to the Spirit so that He who dwells in our spirit may possess all that we are. If we are saved, we have all of the Spirit, but does He have all of you and I?

How many of you would bring a guest into your home and show him into the guest room only to lock him in? If we are saved, the Spirit indwells our spirit, our innermost chamber. What do we do if He steps into the kitchen of our appetites? How do we respond when He opens the closet of our hidden sins? If we deny Him access to any chamber of our lives, we are not giving Him full control of our lives. Remember, the Spirit can be quenched. Is it not amazing that although He is the Almighty God, the Spirit as the heavenly dove does not force Himself on the human will? On the other hand, He is Lord whether or not we recognize Him as such; but in order for us to fully benefit from His lordship, we must yield to Him as Lord.

It is possible to purchase a product and possess the title deed and yet not have the product delivered to us for hands-on possession until a later time. Likewise, when we trusted Christ as Savior, Jesus, who purchased us with His own blood, took the title deed of our life in hand. Romans 12:1 is simply instructing us to deliver to the Spirit of Jesus what He already owns so that He can have full hands-on possession. Since Christ owns us, failing to surrender is really a theft against deity. Surrender is not just an honorable act on our part—it is a responsibility.

For James A. Stewart, like the apostle Paul, this surrender came nearly simultaneously with his salvation. But for many it often comes later, when a person has come to the end of himself not only for salvation but also for sanctification. Usually there is a point of surrender at which the person has, in essence, been saying no to God. For example, when F. B. Meyer was confronted with absolute surrender, he admits that his soul recoiled at the thought. This revealed his lack of surrender beneath the surface. Having supposedly given all to God, he was yet hanging on to one key for one room in his life. Although not finding himself willing, when he finally cried out, "Lord, I'm willing for you to make me willing," he was quickly enabled to give up the issue. That is surrender—giving up! In his yielding, great blessing followed, and F. B. Meyer still impacts many today through his God-blessed writings.

Often surrender is a process that crystallizes to a certain point. It is the point at which a believer, in essence, has been saying no to the Spirit. Many times this is not an obvious issue but rather among the "doubtful things" that truly test surrender. During a meeting on a Monday night, a pastor told me that the night before he had sensed that the Spirit wanted him to give up a particular television program that he and his wife watched regularly on Sunday nights to relax after the Sunday evening service. As the Spirit brought conviction, this issue became a point of surrender. So on that Sunday night, he and his wife gave the program up. He explained to me with joy that he had been aware of the Holy Spirit's reality all day Monday. Surrender had "sensitized" him. By the end of the week long meeting, this pastor had truly experienced personal revival. He cringed as he commented, "I wonder what I would have missed if I had not obeyed the Spirit's leading on Sunday night!"

The point of surrender may differ for you. If it is an ambition that is not God's will for you, give it up. If the Spirit puts His finger on an issue of worldliness in your life that you are savoring—perhaps an area of music or media or clothing—give it up. If there is a spiritually unhealthy relationship in your life, give it up. The issue is not the issues but obeying the Spirit who knows what is best for you. Surrender to the Spirit, and take His will for your life.

This presentation of *all* to the Spirit is the initial entrance into the Spirit-filled life.

Daily Surrender

While the initial presentation of our all is a *directional* surrender, the practice of partnership with the Holy Spirit is an ongoing *daily* surrender. It is the "living sacrifice." The inspired Word issues the command, "Be filled with the Spirit" (Eph. 5:18). The grammatical idea here is a continual yielding to the leadership and power of the Spirit. Literally, "Keep on allowing yourself to be led and empowered by the Spirit." Surrender is a continual responsibility in order for us to access the blessing we received when we got saved. This is a regular reliance upon Christ in us. This is not a once-for-all second blessing but a repeated access of our first blessing!

Some impulsively say, "I'll just let the Spirit take over the steering wheel of my life." But that would take your responsibility out of it, because if He was behind the wheel, everything from then on would be perfect. To use this analogy, as my father often taught, the Spirit would say, "No, you stay behind the wheel. I'll stay over here in the passenger seat. Just do everything I say. Go when I say go. Stop when I say stop. Hold your tongue when I say so. Look away when I prompt you to. Turn that program off when I say so. Forgive when I say forgive. Witness when I tell you to. Speak a kind word when I say so." When we yield to the Holy Spirit's commands, we are yielding to the leadership of the Holy Spirit. In keeping with the analogy, we are the chauffer for the Holy Spirit. We are the chauffer for deity!

When we are driving and someone else is navigating, if we trust our navigator, we simply follow his directions. We don't really think much about it. We just obey because we trust the one giving directions. Likewise, the Holy Spirit is a trustworthy navigator. We must always trust and obey His divine navigation. The Spirit-filled life is not Spirit control in the sense of us being automatons; rather it is Spirit leadership with our cooperation.

We must yield to the Spirit regarding sin and self issues. "Grieve not the Holy Spirit of God" (Eph. 4:30). The grammar can mean "stop grieving the Holy Spirit." Our heavenly partner is a person who can be grieved. What is it that grieves the Holy Spirit? Sin! In fact, the context of the last half of Ephesians 4 includes much admonition against specific sins: stealing, corrupt communication, bitterness, wrath, anger, clamor, evil speaking, and malice, among others. In yielding to the leadership of the Spirit, we must confess all known sin. This does not mean sinless perfection—it means immediate confession as the Holy Spirit convicts of sin. The Spirit will not lead us toward media choices, fashion choices, and music choices that please the devil. Doubtful things must be done away with until we are fully convinced by the Spirit from the Scripture. Otherwise, in the name of "gray areas," we are giving Satan the benefit of the doubt, which most certainly grieves the Spirit. Reconciliation must be sought when we have wronged another and when that person knows it or has a right to know it. Restitution must be made. Self-will must be rejected as we embrace God's will.

We must also yield to the Spirit regarding divine guidance. "Quench not the Spirit" (1 Thess. 5:19). The word "quench" simply means "to extinguish or put out as quenching fire with water." The verb is an imperative. It is a command to every child of God. This implies that it is possible to quench the Spirit and thus hinder our Christian growth. We see, therefore, that spiritual growth is not automatic or inevitable. The grammar can mean "stop quenching the Spirit." When this is the case, the force behind the command is to stop quenching the Spirit of revival. Stop dousing the flame of God's Spirit. Stop putting self over God.

In addition to obeying the negative command, we must positively yield to the Spirit's leadership for each step of the Christian walk. "Walk in the Spirit, and ye shall not fulfil the lust of the flesh. . . . But if ye be led of the Spirit, ye are not under the law" (Gal. 5:16–18). These verses imply that when we follow the leadership of the Spirit, He empowers us to overcome the law of sin. Therefore, always obey with trust; He will never lead us astray. Always say yes to His commands. Remember, the Spirit always works in harmony with the Word. We'll see more about this biblical balance of the Word and the Spirit in another chapter.

For some, "controlled carnality" is preferred to really yielding to the leadership of the Spirit. Corporately, some churches prefer tradition over true surrender to the Spirit as the administrator of the church. This squelches spontaneity in corporate prayer meetings and the Spirit's liberty in public services.

We stop grieving the Spirit by dealing with sin. We stop quenching the Spirit by denying self. We walk in the Spirit by yielding to His leadership and power. Thus, by keeping short accounts through immediate confession and by positively learning to trustfully obey the Spirit's voice, we are yielding to the Spirit as our senior partner. Our lack of willingness on this point holds back revival.

An evangelist from the past, R. Paul Miller, tells the following story:

> During a series of meetings in Iowa, we were
> having hard sledding. Coldness was all around—
> no responses at all. After two weeks of this, on

a Sunday morning the pastor, under tremendous strain, arose and slowly said, "People, I am a failure. I have worked for three years to bring about revival in this community, and I have failed. I must be a mistake in the ministry. I am resigning as pastor this morning. I don't want to stand in God's way here." The audience was astonished. They all liked him.

Then a man, Mr. Williams, on the right side arose and said, "Pastor, I am not surprised that there is no revival here the way Brother Cook and I have been treating each other."

They belonged to different political parties and had allowed it to enter the church. The congregation had gradually taken sides. The church was in a tragic state.

Williams walked across the church to Cook's seat. Cook had an injured foot and couldn't walk. Williams stepped up to Cook and said, "George, I'm ashamed of the things I have said about you. They were false. I'm sorry and want you to forgive me. Will you do it?"

With that, Cook stood up and said, "Howard, you're a better man than I. You came to me. I wasn't man enough to go to you. I apologize for all I have said. Forgive me."

They stood there swaying in each other's arms as the aisle filled with people streaming to the front. THEN we had revival. And what a revival! When revivals fail, someone is to blame.

We must yield to the Spirit as Lord. This gives Him His proper place as the senior partner. To do less is to usurp His position. Healthy partnerships recognize who is who. The

Spirit is the senior partner; therefore we must gladly yield to His leadership. Submission is the way into blessing.

Questions for Personal Reflection

1. Have you presented all in your life to the lordship of the Holy Spirit? If so, when?

2. What sin or self issues is the Holy Spirit convicting you of, if any? Will you make them right by agreeing with God and trusting in the cleansing power of the blood of Jesus?

3. What faith steps is the Holy Spirit leading you to take?

Chapter Five

THE EMPOWERING PARTNER

Samuel Chadwick was zealous for Jesus, but God had more in store for him: the power of the Holy Spirit's fire:

> Samuel Chadwick was born in the industrial north of England in 1860. His father worked long hours in the cotton mill, and when he was only eight Samuel went to work there also to help support his impoverished family.
>
> Devout Methodists, the family attended chapel three times on Sunday, and as a young boy Chadwick gave his heart to Christ. Listening to God's Word week by week, he often felt the inner call to serve Christ. It seemed impossible, as he was poor and uneducated; but in faith he made preparations. After a twelve-hour factory shift, Chadwick would rush home for five hours of prayer and study.
>
> At the age of 21, he was appointed lay pastor of a chapel at Stacksteads, Lancashire. It was no dream appointment; the congregation was self-satisfied. Yet Chadwick threw himself in with great optimism. He had been trained to prepare well-researched and interesting sermons as the sure way to bring in the crowds. He recalled later: "This led unconsciously to a false aim in my work. I lived and labored for my sermons, and was unfortunately more concerned about their excellence and reputation than the repentance of the people."

Soon, however, his sermons were exhausted and nothing had changed. Staring defeat in the face and sensing his lack of real power, he felt an intense hunger kindled within him for more of God. At this point he heard the testimony of someone who had been revitalized by an experience of the Holy Spirit; so with a few friends he covenanted to pray and search the Scriptures until God sent revival.

One evening as he was praying over his next sermon, a powerful sense of conviction settled on him. His pride, blindness and reliance on human methods paraded before his eyes as God humbled him to the dust. Well into the night he wrestled and repented; then he took out his pile of precious sermons and set fire to them! The result was immediate: the Holy Spirit fell upon him. In his own words: "I could not explain what had happened, but it was a bigger thing than I had ever known. There came into my soul a deep peace, a thrilling joy, and a new sense of power. My mind was quickened. I felt I had received a new faculty of understanding. Every power was vitalized. My body was quickened. There was a new sense of spring and vitality, a new power of endurance, and a strong man's exhilaration in big things."

The tide turned. After his next sermon, seven souls were converted ("one for each of my barren years"), and he called the whole congregation to a week of prayer. The following weekend most of the church was baptized in the Holy Spirit, and revival began to spread through the valleys. In the space of a few months, hundreds were converted to Jesus, among them some of the most notorious sinners in the area.[1]

Not everyone may have, or needs to have, as dramatic an experience. But whether immediately dramatic or increasingly dramatic, everyone may know, and needs to know, the power of the Holy Spirit. In fact, this is an absolute necessity for every believer.

Communion with the Holy Spirit in our text in 2 Corinthians 13:14 will also lead us to trust in His power. Since the Spirit is the empowering partner in our relationship with Him, we must depend on His power. We must yield our strength to the strength of another. We must exchange our strength, which is actually weakness, for the Spirit's strength. The Spirit-filled life is not us becoming strong but rather us recognizing that we are weak (and always will be) and casting ourselves on the strong One. This is a life-changing realization. Simply put, we must depend on the Spirit to live His strength through our weak but yielded vessel. This is full surrender.

The Provision of Power

Is there really a provision of supernatural enablement for believers?

The Example of Christ

Christ was conceived of the Holy Spirit (see Matt. 1:20). Just as believers are indwelt by the Spirit at salvation, so Christ was indwelt by the Spirit at conception. He was filled with the Spirit even as a child. "The child grew, and waxed strong in spirit, filled with wisdom: and the grace of

God [Spirit enablement] was upon him" (Luke 2:40). Then, when Christ entered His three years of public ministry, He was baptized. Immediately "the Holy Ghost descended in a bodily shape like a dove upon him" (Luke 3:22).

The next event recorded states, "Jesus being full of the Holy Ghost returned from the Jordan, and was led by the Spirit into the wilderness" (Luke 4:1). There He was victorious over the devil (see Luke 4:2–13). "Jesus returned in the power of the Spirit . . . and He taught" (Luke 4:14–15). In the synagogue in Nazareth, Christ read from Isaiah, "The Spirit of the Lord is upon me, because he hath anointed me to preach" (Luke 4:18). Then He said, "This day is this Scripture fulfilled in your ears," and so on throughout His public ministry.

At His incarnation, in order to become fully man, Jesus took on the limitations of a human body by setting aside the use of the attributes of His inherent deity (see Phil. 2:6–8). Because of this, Christ did all that He did as a man in dependence on the power of the Spirit. In fact, referring to His work on the cross, the Scripture says that Jesus "through the eternal Spirit offered himself without spot to God" (Heb. 9:14).

Christ emptied Himself not of His deity nor of His attributes of deity but of *the use of* His divine attributes. Therefore, He had to depend on the ministry of the Holy Spirit. He set the perfect example of Spirit dependence. If Christ in His humanity needed the ministry of the Holy Spirit, how much more do we?

The Promise of the Spirit

In his sermon on the Day of Pentecost, Peter stated that Christ, "being by the right hand of God exalted, and having received of the Father the promise of the Holy Ghost, . . . shed forth [literally "poured out"] this, which ye now see and hear" (Acts 2:33). What is "the promise of the Holy Spirit"?

Jesus told His disciples to "wait for the promise of the Father" (Acts 1:4), which He had already told them about. Forty-three days earlier in the Upper Room discourse, Christ had repeatedly promised that when He left, He and the Father would send the Spirit. How would the disciples know when this occurred? Christ explained, "Ye shall be baptized with the Holy Ghost" (Acts 1:5). The definite article "the" is actually absent. Therefore Christ is grammatically emphasizing the quality or power of the Holy Spirit. He is emphasizing "Holy Spirit-ness."

In a parallel account, after commissioning His disciples to be witnesses (remember, at that point they were defeated men), Christ said, "Behold, I send the promise of my Father upon you: but tarry ye . . . until ye be endued with power from on high" (Luke 24:49). In both accounts Christ urged His disciples to wait for *the promise*. In Acts He defined this as being "baptized with [the power of] the Holy Spirit." In Luke He defined this as being "endued with power from on high." Therefore the promise of the Spirit is a promise of power!

Factually this occurs at salvation. The Scripture clarifies, "For ye are all the children of God by faith in Christ Jesus. For as many of you as have been baptized into Christ have put on Christ" (Gal. 3:26–27). "Have put on" comes from the word translated in Luke 24:49 "be endued." We already noted that in Acts 1:5 "be endued" is parallel with "be baptized." So when we believed in Christ, not only were we baptized into Christ when the Spirit placed us into Christ, we were also baptized or endued with Christ when Christ placed His Spirit into us. This is a fact for every believer and constitutes a provision of power.

However, functionally, or experientially, this provision must be accessed by faith. We are justified "that we might receive [take] the promise of the Spirit *through faith*" (Gal. 3:14; see also 3:8). Although we are given the indwelling Spirit at salvation, we must take hold of His power by faith. The phrase "that we might receive" shows that this is a responsibility of ours, not something that is inevitable. "Through faith" makes it abundantly clear that faith turns the positional facts, which are an actual provision, into experiential function. We'll say more about this access of faith in a moment. However, let's note first the scriptural commands regarding this responsibility.

The Necessity of Power

The power of the Spirit is a necessity for us, not only

because of our need as seen in the example of Christ and because the power to meet that need has been promised us, but also because Scripture commands us to avail ourselves of this blessed power.

Be Filled with the Spirit

In the command "Be filled with the Spirit" (Eph. 5:18), the definite article "the" is actually absent, indicating an emphasis on the quality or operation of the person. Not only are we to yield to the Spirit's leadership, we must also depend on the Spirit's enablement to follow that leadership. The Spirit not only gives us orders, but when He is depended upon, He empowers us to carry out those very orders. "Where the Spirit of the Lord is [or where the Spirit is Lord], there is liberty" (2 Cor. 3:17). Not just the right to do right but the liberty to do right. This is true Christian liberty. Not the freedom to do as we please but the freedom, or power, to do right. This is liberty indeed!

Spirit enablement accessed by faith liberates our personality for God's service and glory. No longer is our personality animated by mere human life but rather by divine life. This gives a supernatural dynamic to a formerly powerless child of God. This is the revived life. The confusion, however, often comes regarding our ability to fully surrender. Some sincere souls cry out, "I surrender all, and I'm going to do it!" But we cannot live for God in our own power. It is not

His will, our way. If we surrender to the Spirit's leadership but then depend on our own power to attempt to carry it out, we really have not surrendered to His leadership. This leaves the "surrender" empty and powerless, and the believer who does this is left perplexed and discouraged. True surrender depends on the Spirit's leadership *and* His enablement for us to follow His leadership.

Just as one does not believe in Jesus until he depends on Jesus as Savior, so we really do not believe in the Holy Spirit until we are depending on the Holy Spirit for everything. It is when we are that the Spirit of Christ gives us experientially the sufficiency of Christ, which we already possess as a child of God. Surrender—real faith—is the access. As noted in the previous chapter, this is not a second blessing—it is accessing our first blessing.

Some misunderstand the Spirit-filled life to be only Spirit leadership, and they miss the truth that the Spirit-filled life is also Spirit empowerment. If the Spirit-filled life is just Spirit leadership, then "just obey" is the key. But obedience through flesh dependence profits nothing (see John 6:63). Or, if the Spirit-filled life is only Spirit empowerment, then "just trust" is the key. But trusting for what we want is not the same as trusting for what God wants. However, if the Spirit-filled life is a matter of Spirit leadership *and* Spirit empowerment, then "trust to obey" is the key. Certainly we must yield to the Spirit's leadership, but we also must depend on His power to enable us to follow His leading. No one can "just obey" the Word of God without the power of God. God dependence accesses Spirit enablement.

You and I cannot live the Spirit-filled life in our own power. The Spirit-filled life is a Life—a person—living through our yielded, dependent vessel. The Spirit-filled life, the victorious life, the deeper life, the higher life is not a new line of teaching, a mere set of doctrines, a mere set of moral motions, a conference, or a movement; it is a Life—and His name is Jesus! The Spirit of Jesus moved into us to live His life, not ours. As long as we live our life, we will veil His life. But when we stop living our life, He will manifest His life in us. No one can live the Christian life but Christ. But He lives in us so that we can live—yet not us but Christ in us—the Christian life.

Walk in the Spirit

The command to "walk in the Spirit" (Gal. 5:16) implies that this reality is not automatic. We are commanded to *walk*, not simply to sit back and assume that we are Spirit filled. But what does it mean to walk in the Spirit?

The Scripture explains, "As ye have therefore received Christ Jesus the Lord, so walk ye in him" (Col. 2:6). We received Christ by surrendering to the conviction of the Holy Spirit regarding sin, righteousness, and judgment, thus choosing to depend on Christ to save us. So how do we *walk in Him*? How do we *walk in the Spirit*? By surrendering to the Spirit's leadership for the next step and choosing to depend on His power to take that step.

Walking is reiterated steps. Therefore, walking in the Spirit is reiterated steps in the Spirit—reiterated steps of faith. This reveals that partnership with the Spirit is simply one step at a time. We need not look backward, nor should we fear the future. Satan may urge us to look backward perhaps to discourage us with the thought that we are "too bad" to ever be used of God. Or he may urge us to fear the future with the thought that it is only a matter of time, and we will blow it. Either focus can move us from a position of faith. But if we are presently trusting, then the Spirit is presently enabling.

As noted above, this is not a matter of "just obey," because unsaved moralists can go through the motions of outward obedience. Nor is it a matter of "just trust," which is not trust at all but passivity. It is a matter of "trust to obey." God dependence accesses Spirit enablement as the power to actually obey. What a blessing—there is hope! Just as when Jesus told the paralyzed man to take up his bed and walk, an act that was humanly impossible, so when the Spirit of Jesus commands us to think rightly, speak the soft answer, or declare the gospel, it may seem impossible for us to do. But just as the paralyzed man received miraculous strength when he, by faith, reached for the bed, so when we depend on the Spirit for that impossible step, He supernaturally enables us to actually take the step. Victory in Christ is victory without trying. But victory without trying is not victory doing nothing—it is victory with trusting! That demands the step of faith. This is not idle passivity—it is active cooperation.

One dear lady wrote to me to testify of this reality in the matter of the gospel. She had never led a soul to Christ, but she determined to obey the Spirit on this matter and depend on His power to carry it out. When the Spirit prompted her to witness to an unsaved teen girl, she wrote that she was terrified. Thankfully, faith is not a feeling, and when she took the step of faith by opening her mouth, she said it was as if the Holy Spirit just took over. By the second conversation the two had the next day, the girl made a decision to trust Christ as her Savior.

How much would change if we lived the life of surrender, which is the life of faith! What blessings we would experience, what victory in Christ we would access, what joy we would know! Since the Holy Spirit is the empowering partner, we must depend on His power. But how do we do that?

The Access of Power

The access revolves around three simple words: *ask, take,* and *act*. If the goal is to access a present reality (fact), then the key faith steps are simply to *take* and then to *act*, since we do not have to ask for what is already presently provided. If the aim is to access a future potentiality (promise), then the first faith step is to *ask* followed by the faith steps to *take* and then to *act*. Generally speaking, the provision for personal victory is based on facts or present realities, whereas the provision for effective ministry to others is based on promises or future potentialities. Let's use an example that shows how all three faith steps are applied.

Ask

Luke 11:13 is so simple and clear: "If ye then, being evil, know how to give good gifts unto your children: how much more shall your heavenly Father give the Holy Spirit to them that *ask* him?" Some may object that this promise is no longer valid because it was fulfilled on the Day of Pentecost. But Luke inscribed this promise under inspiration long after the Day of Pentecost. Would this glorious promise be inscribed under the inspiration of the Holy Spirit when it was no longer valid? Obviously not; therefore, this promise is for today!

"How much more" indicates that the Father delights in granting this request. The definite article "the" is again absent before the name "Holy Spirit," indicating the quality, operation, or power of the Spirit—*Holy Spirit-ness*. We are to *ask* for the power of the Holy Spirit. Also, "ask" in this verse is in the present tense, indicating continuous action. In other words, asking is not a one-time event but a repeated event. We find this illustrated throughout the book of Acts. In Acts 1:14 the followers of Jesus prayed. In Acts 2:4 they were "filled with the Holy Ghost." In Acts 4 they prayed again, and again they "were all filled with the Holy Ghost, and they spake the word of God with boldness" (Acts 4:31). And so on throughout the book of Acts.

Jesus said *ask*, just simply *ask*! Regardless of our level of understanding, we are to just ask for the power of the Holy Spirit. God will straighten out in us what needs to be adjusted so that He can answer our prayer, for *how much more shall your heavenly Father give [the power of] the Holy Spirit to them that ask Him.*

Take

Acts 1:8 says, "Ye shall receive power, after that the Holy Ghost is come upon you." Here the future tense is used as an imperative much as a parent might say, "You will do this!" The word "receive" is often translated "take." Notice that it does not say "ye shall be given power" but rather "ye shall *receive* power." We are responsible to *take* by faith what we are asking for. The next phrase in Acts 1:8 is difficult to translate. Actually, there is no preposition in it. Awkwardly, but literally, it says "the Holy Spirit coming on you." So we are to ask in faith for the power of the Spirit and then to take by faith the power of the Spirit, regardless of our feelings.

When my son asks me for a piece of candy and I hold one out to him, he always takes it! Likewise, we are simply to ask for the Spirit's power and then simply to take it by faith—because the Father promises to give Holy Spirit-ness to those who ask.

Act

Acts 1:8 then commands, "Ye shall be witnesses unto me." We must *ask*, *take*, and then in faith *act* upon the reality that the Spirit is enabling us. In this passage the step of obedience is witnessing. As we open our mouth to witness or step out in obedience in any other way, the Spirit will enable us for the step of obedience that we are taking. This is trusting to obey. This is partnership with the Spirit of power!

Friendship with the Spirit is not struggling or trying but trusting Christ in us to express His life through our weak but surrendered, dependent channel. When this reality of Galatians 2:20 living was brought home to me, what a difference this partnership began to make in my own personal journey. "I live; yet not I, but Christ liveth in me" by "faith." This dynamic reality is not inevitable but rather by *faith*. Faith is neither a fatalistic passivity nor a flesh-dependent activity, but a God-dependent, Spirit-enabled relationship.

When David O'Gorman, whom I mentioned in chapter 1 of this book, was a fairly new believer studying for the ministry, he was stirred with the promise of Luke 11:13. Early in his ministry, he preached the simple truth of the verse. But at that time an older preacher told him that Luke 11:13 was not for today. As a young preacher, David's faith was undermined.

This led him to sincere but frustrated ministry. But during the revival mentioned in chapter 1, God brought him back to faith regarding the promise of Luke 11:13. Since then the difference that trusting for divine unction has made in his life and ministry is like the difference between night and day.

The same will be true for you. Simply *ask*, *take*, and *act*. As you do, God will manifest His divine life through the surrendered, dependent channel of your life.

Questions for Personal Reflection

1. In what ways are you aware of the necessity of the Holy Spirit's power?

2. What biblical *commands* indicate that the Spirit-empowered life is not merely a suggestion but a necessity?

3. What faith steps should you apply to begin accessing the Spirit's provision of power?

Chapter Six

A SACRED TRUST

Downtown Chicago is a favorite spot for my wife and I to visit. One winter we walked down Michigan Avenue. For the fun of it, I suggested that we go into one of the really high-end stores. When I saw long fur coats not only on the mannequins but also on the customers, I realized that we were in the wrong place!

In stores such as this, several things are observable in the jewelry section. Valuable jewels remain encased under lock and key. Small cameras keep a watchful eye on browsing customers. Also, a man in uniform, armed with a gun, makes his presence known. Clearly these kinds of stores are guarding something that they consider valuable. In like manner, we must guard our friendship with the Holy Spirit, which is more valuable than any jewel.

Acts 2:33 declares that Jesus, "being by the right hand of God exalted, and having received of the Father the promise of the Holy Ghost, . . . shed forth [poured out] this, which ye now see and hear." On the Day of Pentecost, Christ sent the Spirit—and the Spirit has not been sent back. This reality allows for the truth of 2 Corinthians 13:14, which we've been contemplating in the last four chapters, to take place. We can actually have *communion* with the Holy Spirit.

But this entails a great responsibility. Since we live in the dispensation of the Spirit, we must guard this friendship that we have with the Holy Spirit.

The Dispensations of the Godhead

When reading true classics on the Holy Spirit, one will most certainly be blessed in reading J. Elder Cumming's *Through the Eternal Spirit*, Handley Moule's *The Holy Spirit*, and A. J. Gordon's *The Ministry of the Spirit*. Later writers often quote from these works. All three emanate with reverence and biblical precision on the subject of the Holy Spirit. Both Moule and Gordon refer to a concept that we might term "the dispensations of the Godhead." Each of these divine dispensations dictates, as it were, a divine test of living orthodoxy—a particular emphasis on how people were to relate to God in the way that He revealed Himself in that era. Satan's attack on God's people, then, always parallels the emphasis of each dispensation. Note the following distinctions.

The Dispensation of the Father

The Old Testament could be termed "the dispensation of the Father." The person of God the Father clearly is in prominence in this era. The emphasis is on the oneness of God. Therefore the test of living orthodoxy for the people of God during that dispensation was to regard that emphasis.

Consequently, Satan's attack was on that very point. Do we not read repeatedly of Israel's great sin of idolatry?

The Dispensation of the Son

Christ's coming to earth at the first advent might be termed "the dispensation of the Son." It will not be His only dispensation. As we read the Gospels, clearly God the Son is seen in prominence. The test of living orthodoxy for the people of God revolved around Jesus Christ. Would those who were orthodox regarding the Father now properly receive and relate to the Son? Therefore, Satan's attack on God's people shifted to the Son. What does the Scripture say? "He came unto his own, and his own received him not" (John 1:11).

The Dispensation of the Holy Spirit

Christ finished His glorious work at Calvary and ascended to the right hand of the throne of power. There He received the promise of the Spirit and then sent the Holy Spirit to His followers. This event launched what may be termed "the dispensation of the Holy Spirit." Since the Holy Spirit has not yet been sent back, we today live in the age of the Holy Spirit. The Spirit is the administrator of the church age. The test of living orthodoxy today for God's people regards the Holy Spirit. Will those who are orthodox regarding the Father and the Son now properly receive and relate to the

Spirit? Therefore, Satan's attack on God's people has shifted to this very point.

In the messages sent to the churches of this age recorded in Revelation 2–3, the Scripture repeatedly says, "He that hath an ear, let him hear what the Spirit saith unto the churches." Although Jesus Christ is speaking, notice how He emphasizes *the Spirit* speaking to the churches. This point emphasizes the present dispensation of the Spirit.

At the beginning of the dispensation of the Spirit, is it not significant that when Ananias sinned, Peter said, "Why hath Satan filled thine heart to lie to the Holy Ghost?" (Acts 5:3). Notice Satan's attack, and notice that the lie was directly against the Holy Spirit. Why did Peter not say the Father or the Son? Because this is the age or dispensation of the Spirit, and inspiration here clearly portrays this very point.

The Present Attack: Strange Fire and No Fire

Over these past two thousand years, Satan has persisted with this attack. Although the attack among the lost revolves around all three persons of the Godhead, the attack among the saints pertains primarily to the Holy Spirit. In light of what we have just noted, this should not surprise us.

Consequently, many refer to the Holy Spirit as "it." Many attempt service for Christ without seeking the leadership of the Spirit or without depending on Him for effective service. Some focus on the gifts of the Spirit instead of the God of the gifts. Some embrace counterfeits of the Spirit. Satan has done all he can to keep the saints from a right understanding of and relationship to the Holy Spirit.

James A. Stewart, a missionary evangelist from Scotland who saw revival repeatedly during his itinerate lifetime, wrote a book on the ministry of the Holy Spirit entitled *Heaven's Throne Gift*. He wrote this book before the Charismatic movement of the 1960s. In the book he points out that any group of fundamentalist preachers would agree regarding God the Father and God the Son. But, he continues, they would disagree regarding God the Spirit, and the disagreement would in some cases be so sharp that fellowship would be strained and some would accuse others of false doctrine.[1]

Then the 1960s brought the Charismatic explosion, which took elements of Pentecostal thinking across denominational lines. Although there were and are many sincere brethren within this movement who have a real walk with God, biblical fundamentalists and conservative evangelicals rightly rejected the *excesses* of the movement. Truly there are excesses that reveal the mark of satanic deception or show the marks of fleshly imitation. The resulting dual streams of power weaken or discredit real fire. However, I fear that in the understandable and needed reaction against strange fire, there has been an overreaction to it that embraces no fire. Orthodoxy without the life of the Spirit is dead orthodoxy.

Satan knows that a believer who is not rightly related to the Holy Spirit is powerless.

Some today, in their desire to put out strange fire, have deemphasized biblical subjectivism, which is the real, interactive ministry of the Holy Spirit based on biblical truth. This leads to sheer objectivism. My father, Wayne Van Gelderen, Sr., used to say, "Pure objectivism is one step away from liberalism." Liberalism denies the supernatural, while pure objectivism minimizes the supernatural. Therefore, pure objectivism is one step away from liberalism. On the other hand, pure subjectivism is also one step away from liberalism. Liberalism denies the inerrant, divine revelation, while pure subjectivism minimizes it. Therefore, pure subjectivism is also one step away. The key is the Word (objective truth) and the Spirit (subjective truth based on objective truth) in operation together. Jesus said that we must "worship him [God] in spirit and in truth" (John 4:24). The Spirit without the Word is delusion. The Word without the Spirit is deadness. But the combination of the Word and the Spirit is dynamic!

Some today minimize any specific leading of the Spirit and simply point to the Word. However, this ignores the reality of *communion* with the Spirit. Also, this thinking practically denies the personality of the Spirit. While strange fire (in the name of the Spirit) must be rejected, no fire (in the name of the Word) is not the answer. The key is the Word *and* the

Spirit. The Spirit always works in harmony with the Word. The legitimate subjective realm is according to the objective boundaries of the Word. Therefore, on the one hand, we must not allow deadness to lead us to overreact and embrace delusion, and on the other hand, we must not allow strange fire to lead us to overreact and embrace no fire.

Some note the parallel between Ephesians 5:18–19, "Be filled with the Spirit; speaking to yourselves in psalms and hymns and spiritual songs, singing and making melody in your heart to the Lord," and Colossians 3:16, "Let the word of Christ dwell in you richly in all wisdom; teaching and admonishing one another in psalms and hymns and spiritual songs, singing with grace in your hearts to the Lord." They then argue that the Word is most important, not the Spirit. But this same kind of logic could argue that the Spirit is most important, not the Word. Is it not obvious that the Bible emphasizes the Word *and* and the Spirit?

Some argue that we do not need to surrender to the Spirit— we just need to surrender to the Word. But who authored the Word through the biblical writers, and who illumines and convinces us of the Word? The Spirit. Cannot we see the vital importance of both? The Scripture explains, "The letter killeth, but the spirit giveth life" (2 Cor. 3:6). The issue is not the Word *or* the Spirit but the Word *and* the Spirit.

In all this we can note a subtle apostasy (falling away) within conservative Christianity. Full-blown apostasy in doctrine often begins with an apostasy in practice. On the one hand, in de-emphasizing the Holy Spirit, some have unwittingly begun a subtle apostasy in practice (no experience). On the other hand, some who have recognized deadness and powerlessness have sadly embraced a counterfeit life. When worldliness and carnal conduct is ignored or even embraced as a marketing tool, there has also been an apostasy in practice (false experience). Eventually apostasy in doctrine often follows. In both cases, where does the apostasy begin? It begins with a falling away from a right relationship with the Holy Spirit. This is the cause for powerlessness and worldliness. This subtle apostasy from the Holy Spirit's person and power leads to apostasy in practice, which leads to apostasy in doctrine.

Furthermore, as Moule (quoting John Owen) acknowledges in his book, neglecting the ministry of the Holy Spirit today is on the same level as Israel's idolatry in the Old Testament and the Jews' rejection of the Messiah.[2] Slighting the Holy Spirit today is slighting Christ's throne gift for this age. The sent Spirit of the glorified Christ is the gift of the Spirit from Christ for this dispensation. Is it not alarming that sound fundamental people today have played right into Satan's deceptive tactics? In running from the wild fire of others, some have stumbled right into the trap of subtle apostasy from the Holy Spirit by deemphasizing the Spirit. Yet it is the Spirit who indwells believers to enable those who trust

Him to do the work of God. As A. W. Tozer said, "The Holy Spirit is the cure for fanaticism, not the cause of it."[3]

The Key Protection: the Word of God

The major protection we have for guarding our relationship with the Holy Spirit from strange fire is the Word of God. The Spirit without the Word is not the Spirit—it is delusion. This is what leads to strange fire. "The Spirit of truth" (John 14:17; 15:26; 16:13) will always work according to the Word of truth (see John 17:17). The Spirit as the author of Scripture (see 2 Pet. 1:21) will not violate Himself. Therefore, Holy Spirit leadership is always in harmony with the principles of God's Word. The Spirit never speaks contrary to the Word. The Spirit will never lead us to do wrong in order for us to gain an opportunity to do right. Also, it is dangerous for us to trust impressions alone, for Satan is a deceiver. The truth of biblical principle is the key to discerning the error of satanic counterfeits. We will address this matter of discerning true guidance from false guidance in the next chapter.

Every Spirit-filled believer must of necessity be Word filled. For we cannot access the Spirit except by faith, which has the Word as its foundation. However, some may learn the Word merely on the intellectual level but then not depend on it. Without faith, therefore, these people are not Spirit filled. But every Spirit-filled believer must of necessity be Word filled.

Lack of grounding in the Word regarding the Holy Spirit allows Satan to quickly counterfeit real fire and quench real revival. Those who embrace counterfeits may be sincere and even surrendered to the supernatural realm. But if they do not discern between the Holy Spirit and evil spirits, they can be grossly deceived. Imitation is also counterfeit and must be rejected based on the revealed Word of truth. However, real fire must be accepted based on that same Word of truth. It is the Word that instructs us in the legitimate and needful realm of the Holy Spirit. The Word of God is the key protection against both strange fire and no fire.

For many, their partnership with the Spirit is a dysfunctional relationship. Much of this occurs because of a lack of heeding Christ's own teaching—His Word—regarding His Spirit. Jesus says, "If ye had known me, ye should have known my Father also: and from henceforth ye know him, and have seen him" (John 14:7). The phrase "ye know him" indicates that the disciples knew the Father because they knew the Son. A few verses later Jesus says, "I will pray the Father, and he shall give you another Comforter, that he may abide with you for ever; even the Spirit of truth; whom the world cannot receive, because it seeth him not, neither knoweth him: but ye know him; for he dwelleth with you, and shall be in you" (John 14:16–17). Jesus again uses the phrase "ye know him," this time referring to the Spirit. When Christ then emphasizes, the Spirit "shall be in you," He explains in the next verse, "I will not leave you comfortless: I will come to you." As noted in previous chapters, the Spirit in us is Christ in us! Therefore to ignore, neglect, slight, or despise the Holy Spirit today, even if well intentioned, is actually to ignore, neglect, slight, or despise Christ. Oh, that God's people would wake up to the blessed coming of Christ to them through the Holy Spirit!

No wonder Jesus says, "It is expedient for you [to your advantage] that I go away: for if I go not away, the Comforter will not come unto you; but if I depart, I will send him unto you" (John 16:7). When Christ walked on earth, He could be in only one place at a time because of the limitations of His human body; but by ascending and sending His Spirit, He could now be personally with each disciple everywhere at all times. Not only would the Spirit of Christ dwell *with* each disciple, He would dwell *in* each disciple. As Duncan Campbell put it, this is "deity incorporated into human personality." What a blessed plan of God! This is friendship with the Holy Spirit.

Will you guard your friendship with the Holy Spirit? Without that vibrant partnership, you are powerless and ineffective in the cause of Christ

Questions for Personal Reflection

1. In the present dispensation, which person of the Godhead has been under the greatest attack among believers in Jesus?

2. In what two ways has this attack manifested itself?

3. What objective source provides our key protection from error in this matter?

Chapter Seven

A SPIRITUAL GUIDE

Since Satan knows that a believer who is rightly related to the Holy Spirit is a threat to what he thinks is his turf, he has attacked the person and work of the Holy Spirit. As a result, some today even deny the specific leading of the Holy Spirit. Is this denial valid, or is it perhaps another example of overreacting to the excesses of others? While it is sadly true that some do foolish things in the name of "God led me," do these excesses invalidate what the Scripture teaches regarding divine guidance? What does the Bible teach? We must know the biblical guidelines to Holy Spirit guidance in order to be protected from deception by the enemy and to keep our friendship with the Holy Spirit vibrant.

Does the Holy Spirit provide specific guidance to individual believers? If so, how does He lead? Furthermore, how can we discern counterfeit guidance? We will follow the progression of these three questions throughout this chapter.

Does the Holy Spirit Guide Individually?

Jesus taught the specific leading of the Spirit. Referring to times of persecution, Jesus says, "When they deliver you up, take no thought how or what ye shall speak: for it shall be given you in that same hour what ye shall speak. For it is not ye that speak, but *the Spirit of your Father which speaketh in you*" (Matt. 10:19–20), and, "When they bring you unto the synagogues, and unto magistrates, and powers, take ye no thought how or what thing ye shall answer, or what ye shall say: for *the Holy Ghost shall teach you* in the same hour what ye ought to say" (Luke 12:11–12). The Holy Spirit does specifically lead and empower.

The narrative of Acts demonstrates the specific guidance of the Spirit. When Philip saw the eunuch from Ethiopia on the desert road, "*the Spirit said unto Philip*, Go near, and join thyself to this chariot" (Acts 8:29). This led to the eunuch's conversion. Clearly, the Holy Spirit specifically led Philip to witness to the eunuch, whose heart had been prepared for the message of Jesus.

After Peter saw the vision in Joppa, "while Peter thought on the vision, *the Spirit said unto him*, Behold, three men seek thee. Arise therefore, and get thee down, and go with them, doubting nothing: for I have sent them" (Acts 10:19–20). This led to the conversion of Cornelius and his household, which opened the door to the Gentile harvest. Again, the Spirit specifically led.

During a time of prayer and fasting in the church in Antioch, "as they ministered to the Lord, and fasted, *the Holy Ghost said*, Separate me Barnabas and Saul for the work whereunto I have called them" (Acts 13:2). This led to the first missionary journey, the ingathering of multiple

Gentile converts and a number of churches being started. The Spirit specifically led again.

When Paul and his team would have spent time in Asia, they "were *forbidden of the Holy Ghost* to preach the word in Asia" (Acts 16:6). This was to help lead them to the Macedonian harvest. All these examples illustrate the Spirit's specific leading. Ironically, if Satan could prompt Ananias (see Acts 5:3), then certainly the Holy Spirit can prompt believers.

The Epistles explicitly articulate being "led by the Spirit" (Rom. 8:14) and being "led of the Spirit" (Gal. 5:18). Because He is the "spirit of wisdom" (Eph. 1:17), obviously the Spirit gives wisdom.

Truly, based on biblical truth, there exists a specific leading of the Spirit. To deny the plain sense of these passages involves exegetical straining. There is no reason to believe that the Spirit led individuals in New Testament times any differently than He leads individuals now. Just because some may follow their own whims or a satanic counterfeit does not mean there is not a real leading of the Holy Spirit. How could we "try the spirits," as 1 John 4:1 tells us to, if there is no genuine leading of the Spirit?

The objective Word teaches the subjective reality of the Holy Spirit's leadership. This is an "objective subjectivism." There is an objective biblical basis for the subjective leading of the Holy Spirit. The key is for us to stay within the biblical boundaries, as we noted in the previous chapter.

How Does the Holy Spirit Lead?

How can you know the difference between your own human whims (the flesh) and the Holy Wind of God (the Spirit)? Two key biblical principles provide us a plumb line for discerning how the Spirit leads.

First, there is *the wisdom of the Spirit*, in which the ultimate faculty addressed is our *mind*. This involves a spiritual illumination of the Word to our mind and at the same time a spiritual invigoration of our mind with the Word. When the Holy Spirit reveals to us the grand realities of truth that connect to the inscribed words of Scripture, we "see" truth. He, as the Spirit of truth, guides us into all truth (see John 16:13). He, as the Spirit of wisdom, reveals the knowledge of Christ and enlightens the eyes of our understanding so that we know the riches of God's provision for us (see Eph. 1:17 and following verses). He, as the "eye-opener," opens our eyes so that we may see wonderful things in God's Word (see Ps. 119:18). This illumination of the Word to our mind causes the invigoration of our mind with the Word, and thus, a renewing in the spirit of our mind (see Eph. 4:23).

The foundational principle of guidance is found in this combination of the Word and the Spirit. The food of faith is the Word, for "faith cometh by hearing, and hearing by the word of God" (Rom. 10:17). As the Spirit guides us into truth and opens the eyes of our understanding, He is authoring faith as we look unto Jesus (see Heb. 12:2), who is at oneness with the Word. So if we desire the Holy Spirit to speak to us, we need to delve into the written Word of God, trusting the Spirit to speak the truth to our heart.

This wisdom of the Spirit is real for any child of God who seeks God in His Word. When the Spirit bestows wisdom by making the Word of God come alive to us and thus revealing to our hearts the living Word, He is secondarily demonstrating how He speaks and leads. Learning the Spirit's voice in connection with the Word as the Spirit makes the Word come alive to us provides us an association for discerning the Spirit's voice in any guidance.

Second, there is *the witness of the Spirit*, in which the primary faculty addressed is our *spirit*. This involves communication given to our spirit in conjunction with our mind and at the same time knowledge given to our mind in conjunction with our spirit. But it is primarily Spirit-to-spirit communication, which then works out through our mind. For example, the Spirit bears "witness with our spirit," which is His primary level of communication to us in the realm of our spirit, "that we are the children of God," which is His secondary level of communication with us in the realm of our mind (Rom. 8:16). This is more a matter of knowing than of feeling. It is not that we *feel like* children of God but rather that the Spirit bears witness with our spirit that we *are* children of God. This is a deep knowledge on the spirit level, not merely a feeling that may come and go on the soul level. As the convincer (see John 16:8), the Holy Spirit convinces so that we know—from the spirit to our mind—that we know.

The Spirit speaking so that we *know* is pictured in several ways. First, when the Spirit leads, there is a sense of light with no darkness, because "God is light, and in him is no darkness at all" (1 John 1:5). The Spirit's leading is clear. It is accompanied by light. It is not hazy and confusing. Second, when the Spirit guides, there is a sense of life with no deadness, because "the letter killeth, but the spirit giveth life" (2 Cor. 3:6). The Spirit's leading is full of life and vitality. It is not "dry bones." Third, when the Spirit leads, there is a sense of liberty with no duress, because "where the Spirit of the Lord is, there is liberty" (2 Cor. 3:17). The Spirit's leading is liberating. There is freedom. It is not a feeling of bondage or being forced into something.

For example, consider a preacher preparing a sermon. If he has a notion that he is to prepare a certain message, but as he studies, he finds that everything is dry and tedious and there is no sense of freshness—that would be darkness, deadness, and duress. If it is dry and tedious for him in the preparation, it will be worse for the audience! But if as he studies, truth comes alive, and there is meat on the bones and a sense that the message is the need of the hour—that would be light, life, and liberty. If the preacher is enriched in his study, then the audience will be blessed by the overflow—because it is the work of the Spirit.

Learn to read your spirit and recognize the "lift" that comes from true Holy Spirit guidance. Charlie Kittrell, to whom this book is dedicated, often said, "I sense in my spirit . . ." He had learned to discern his spirit and recognize the Holy Spirit's guidance.

Whether we are considering the wisdom of the Spirit or the witness of the Spirit, the Holy Spirit is the convincer, who so convinces us that we begin to know something. This wonderful reality is, of course, based more on the Spirit's ability to speak than on our ability to hear. Still, we must have ears to hear, or we may miss the Spirit's communication.

Sometimes both the wisdom of the Spirit and the witness of the Spirit are involved in a given matter of guidance. However, sometimes there is no witness of the Spirit in a given situation. If we always have to have the witness of the Spirit, then what need is there of the mind? In such cases God has already given light to the mind, which is all that is needed. When the Spirit has been clear through the written Word, there is no need for us to ask for any further guidance that could differ from the Word. If we do ask at that point, it indicates a lack of submission on our part to the Word of God and gives ground for the enemy to provide a false guidance that would contradict the written Word.

How Can We Discern Counterfeit Guidance?

Since Satan can disguise himself as an angel of light (see 2 Cor. 11:14), how can we discern the true from the false? Thankfully, we are not ignorant of Satan's devices (see 2 Cor. 2:11). Knowing the genuine is vital to discerning the counterfeit. Knowing the truth of biblical principle is the key to discerning the error of satanic counterfeits.[1] Therefore, let's note the ways of the Spirit in genuine guidance as an aid to discerning the ways of evil spirits in counterfeit guidance.

First, the Holy Spirit *leads*; evil spirits push. The New Testament describes those who are led by the Spirit (see Rom. 8:14; Gal. 5:18). From it we learn that any guidance that drives, pushes, or even nags like a bug buzzing in your ear is counterfeit. This "pushing" can drive people into excessiveness, which is also a sign of the enemy. Though the Spirit can speak with urgency, counterfeit guidance rushes; it does not allow us time to "try the spirits whether they are of God" (1 John 4:1). If there is no time to obey the command to test the spirits, the guidance is not from the Holy Spirit. When the Spirit speaks, there will be a growing conviction, or "convincement." While impulsiveness is a sign of the flesh, compulsiveness is a sign of satanic counterfeit.

In regard to the conscience, remember that while the conscience is a wonderful God-given aid, it can be misinformed and, therefore, misguided. We must recognize the difference between a law-goaded conscience, which is bondage, and a Spirit-guided conscience, which is liberty. The Holy Spirit leads with a real sense of light, life, and liberty, whereas counterfeit guidance goads.

Second, the Holy Spirit *imparts peace*; evil spirits agitate. "The fruit of the Spirit is . . . peace" (Gal. 5:22). "Let the peace of God rule in your hearts" (Col. 3:15). "God is not the author of confusion, but of peace" (1 Cor. 14:33). The Spirit's peace emanates from the spirit level of our being as a deep knowledge based on truth. Counterfeit peace is feeling that is oriented merely on the soul level and has a tendency to vacillate—which is not peace. Holy Spirit leadership involves the light, life, and liberty of peace. True peace is steady and sure. Counterfeit guidance prompts in a confusing haphazard fashion that irritates and eliminates peace by causing one to leave his position of resting in Christ. Confusion is a sign of counterfeit.

Third, the Holy Spirit communicates initially with our *innermost being*, which is an inner-man appeal; evil spirits approach from our circumference, which is an outer-man appeal. "The Spirit" bears "witness with our spirit" (Rom. 8:16). When the Holy Spirit speaks to us, He speaks to our innermost being. Knowing this helps us to discern the counterfeit guidance that comes from the circumference of our being or, we might say, our outer man rather than our inner man.

How can we discern the difference between the center of our being and the circumference of our being? Think back to a time when you believe that God led you to trust Him for something, and God clearly brought it to pass. That would have been based on true Spirit-to-spirit communication in the center of your being. Compare that to a time when you believe that God led you to trust Him for something, and it clearly did not come to pass. That would have been based on a counterfeit impression from the circumference of your being. We need to recognize the difference between the deep knowing in the center of our being that is from the Spirit and the more surface impression from the circumference of our being that is counterfeit. This will help us to discern the true from the false.

Also, in keeping with this principle of inner man versus outer man, outside audible voices in the *physical* sense, or physical manifestations, are a sign of counterfeit. Although they are "real" experiences, they are false experiences. This differs from *spiritual* hearing or seeing. For example, Elisha prayed that God would open the eyes of his servant to see the horses and chariots of fire in God's army, and God opened his eyes (see 2 Kings 6:15–17). Up to that point all the servant had seen was the enemy. Therefore, the horses and chariots of God were not physical; otherwise, the servant would have seen them. They were spiritual. When there is a true spiritual seeing or hearing, not everyone in the vicinity may see or hear, because it is not physical but spiritual. My grandmother, who exercised simple childlike faith and saw God-glorifying answers to prayer, testified that Jesus often spoke to her—that she heard His voice. Yet if I had been there, I might not have heard anything, because His voice was spiritual, not physical.

Fourth, the Holy Spirit leads through *active cooperation*; evil spirits take advantage of a passive instrument. Commands like "Walk in the Spirit" (Gal. 5:16) and "Quench not the Spirit" (1 Thess. 5:19) demand the active cooperation of our faith. In other words, the Holy Spirit works through our cooperating faculties, while evil spirits work around them. Passivity, especially of the mind and the will, is a playground for the enemy. This is why hypnosis, drug use, and other mind-altering behaviors are so dangerous. God does not violate the human will—and He does not allow evil spirits to either. That is why the Scripture says, "Neither give place to the devil" (Eph. 4:27). Evil spirits cannot "take place" unless you "give place." Flesh indulgence gives place to the devil, since the devil works through the flesh (see Eph. 2:2–3). But regarding counterfeit guidance, when believers will their minds or their wills to be in a passive condition, perhaps through substance abuse, for example, this also gives place to the powers of darkness, which can then take advantage of the situation. In contrast, the Holy Spirit uses our minds, wills, and bodies in a cooperative partnership, which is not passivity.

Beware of times in which guidance comes to you when you are in a "groggy" condition. More than likely this is counterfeit coming from your outer man. When I was younger in my Christian journey, I was perplexed when a particular promise that I believed God had given me did not come to pass. But it "was given" at a time when I was in a "half-in, half-out" condition.

Guidance coming from the Holy Spirit works out through our normal thinking processes. Working from the inside out, the Holy Spirit as "the spirit of [our] mind" (Eph. 4:23) works outward from our spirit through our mind, indicating that the Spirit works through our thinking, not around it. Counterfeit guidance bypasses the normal function of the thinking process. If an impression is presented to our mind like a sudden burst of light and therefore sidesteps our normal thinking process, we should reject it as a counterfeit.

Fifth, the Holy Spirit works in *perfect harmony with the revealed Word of God*; counterfeit guidance compiles arguments that seem to be in line with Scripture but overlooks the points at which this supposed will of God violates a clear truth within the Word of God. This may tempt us to be blind to an explicit truth, since so much else seems right. But if one point does not match up with clearly revealed truth in the Word of God, then the guidance is not from God.

Also, when the Holy Spirit guides through Scripture texts, He does so in their germane sense; counterfeit guidance seeks to use a text outside the principle involved. This misuse of Scripture contradicts other texts of Scripture, as seen in the temptation of Christ (see Matt. 4:1–11; Luke 4:1–13).

Sixth, the Holy Spirit places the *focus on Jesus Christ*; counterfeit guidance places the focus on man—often our own selves. This man-centered focus appeals to our pride. But the Spirit testifies of the Son and glorifies the Son (see John 15:26; 16:14). If we have some great vision of what we think God desires to do, and we find ourselves to be in the limelight of the coming move of God, we're deceived. When I first learned this principle, my balloon of vision burst!

Seventh, Holy Spirit guidance regarding conviction is *specific* and has as its goal cleansing and victory in Christ (see 1 John 1:7, 9); counterfeit conviction is general. When the Holy Spirit convicts us of that which grieves Him, we will know exactly what He is pointing to so that we can confess our *sins*. Counterfeit conviction is just a general impression.

Why would evil spirits seek to "convict" us as believers? Their goal is to get us to begin following the wrong voice. In order to do this, the guidance has to look good. When this foothold is secured, eventually they can lead us along to a point at which our testimony is hurt and disrepute is brought to the cause of Christ.

Eighth, Holy Spirit guidance regarding conviction *edifies*

as it offers hope to those who are broken before the Lord (see 1 John 1:7, 9; Isa. 57:15); counterfeit conviction discourages and has as its goal despair by accusing the brethren (see Rev. 12:10). Any conviction that prompts us to throw in the towel is not from God. We must recognize feelings of discouragement and despair as from the enemy.

Finally, the Holy Spirit leads *practically*; counterfeit guidance is strained and impractical. The Holy Spirit is practical, just as Jesus was when He lived on earth, for the Spirit is "the Spirit of Jesus Christ" (Phil. 1:19). Whenever we are pressed and have to strain to nearly force a matter, it is a sign that the Spirit is not in it. "Where the Spirit of the Lord is, there is liberty" (2 Cor. 3:17). The Holy Spirit is practical.

These examples demonstrate how the objective realm of the Word provides the parameters in which the subjective realm of the Spirit operates. Discerning Christians test the spirits according to biblical principle and then judge righteously. It is vital for us to biblically distinguish the ways of the Holy Spirit versus the ways of evil spirits.

Importance

The spiritual realm is the realm of spirits. When we begin to walk in the Spirit with understanding, we enter more consistently into the *spirit*-ual realm. Therefore, Satan must switch his attacks from merely the physical realm—the flesh or the world—to the spiritual realm. It is vital for believers who begin to live the Spirit-filled life to be ready for this new attack and to be armed with the armor of God, which is essentially putting on Christ—truth, righteousness, peace, (the author of) faith, deliverance, and the Word (see Eph. 6:10–18).

The phrase "in the heavenly places," which speaks of the place where Christ sits far above the enemy (see Eph. 1:20–21), is translated from the same words rendered "in high places," wherein are "spiritual [hosts of] wickedness" (Eph. 6:12). Therefore, in the supernatural realm we must discern between the Holy Spirit and evil spirits, or we can be greatly deceived. If we are truly surrendered but do not understand that in the supernatural realm there is the Holy Spirit as well as evil spirits, we may embrace anything in that realm as if it were the Holy Spirit—for the sake of being surrendered. In this way the enemy may eventually lead us, even though we mean well, to discredit the cause of Christ. This caution must be understood and heeded by seekers of a real relationship with the Holy Spirit. Surrendered but deceived believers unwittingly allow what some call "dual streams." This muddies the clear stream of the Holy Spirit and can hinder real revival.

If we do get something wrong—and we all do at times— then we need to admit that we got it wrong. To fail to do so only increases the deception. Not being teachable is a sign of deception. Just say, "Lord, You didn't get it wrong—I did. Give me greater discernment for the future." Thankfully, if we trust the Holy Spirit to grow our level of discernment, He will. Over time and sometimes learning the hard way, we will mature in our spiritual discernment. Embracing truth dispels error. Trust your spiritual guide—the Holy Spirit, the Spirit of truth.

Questions for Personal Reflection

1. What scriptural truths have come alive to you, thus showing you how to recognize the Spirit's voice?
2. In what ways have you followed the Holy Spirit's specific leadership in your life?
3. In what ways have you followed counterfeit guidance?

Chapter Eight

THE REVIVAL RELATIONSHIP

The grace of the Lord Jesus Christ, and the love
of God, and the communion of the Holy Ghost,
be with you all. Amen.
2 Corinthians 13:14

Communion with the Holy Spirit—is this real in your life? What is the Holy Spirit to you? What does the Spirit mean to you? How is your relationship with the Holy Spirit? Do you have a vibrant friendship with the Spirit? We began our study with these questions. Since then we have been investigating what it means to live in partnership with the Holy Spirit.

Since we are to commune with the Holy Spirit, we must develop a friendship with our heavenly partner. In order for us, as the human partner, to properly relate with the Spirit as the heavenly partner, we must know who He is to us personally. We've seen that the Spirit is the divine partner. As such, we must honor Him as God. We've seen that He is a personal partner. As such, we must treat Him as a person. We've noted that the Spirit is clearly the senior partner. As such, we must yield to Him as Lord. We've seen that the Spirit is the empowering partner. As such, we must depend on Him for enablement. We've also investigated the dispensation of the Spirit in which we live right now. Therefore, we must guard our relationship with the Spirit from Satan's insidious attack. Further, we have addressed how to discern genuine Holy Spirit guidance from counterfeit guidance.

When we know the Spirit as God, treat the Spirit as a person, yield to the Spirit as Lord by surrendering to His leadership and depending on His enablement, and carefully guard this friendship with discernment, we have entered into the revival relationship. "Revive" means "life again." "Re" ("again") plus "vive" ("life") equals a restoration to life. To be revived physically is to be restored to physical life. To be revived spiritually is to be restored to spiritual life—life in the Spirit. Revival, whether personal or corporate, always restores individuals to a right relationship with the Holy Spirit. This is friendship with the Spirit. It is the Spirit-filled life for holiness and service. Will you live in the reality of your friendship with the Spirit through faith?

Let's finish the story we began about Walter Wilson back at the end of chapter 1. Wilson, you may remember, had been taught that he should not expect spiritual fruit and that He should never pray directly to the Holy Spirit, and as a result, his ministry had been dry and barren. Through the kind confrontation of a man of God, Wilson had become desirous "to know the Spirit and to serve Him successfully." From his book on the Holy Spirit, *Ye Know Him*, he relates the rest of the story:

About this time the Lord very graciously sent a devoted minister from Chicago who brought a wonderful message on Romans 12:1. Having finished his address on the subject, he leaned over the pulpit and said, "It is the Holy Spirit to whom you are to give your body. Your body is the temple of the Holy Spirit, and you are requested in this passage to give it to Him for His possession. Will you do this tonight?"

I left the service deeply impressed with the thought that no doubt here was the answer to my deep need and the relief from my barren life. Upon arriving home I went to my study and laid myself flat on the carpet with my Bible open at Romans 12:1. Placing my finger on the passage, I said to the Holy Spirit, "Never before have I come to you with myself: I do so now. You may have my body, my lips, my feet, my brain, my hands, and all that I am and have. My body is yours for you to live within and do as you please. Just now I make you my Lord and I receive you as my own personal God. I shall see your wonderful working in my life, and I know you will make Christ very real to my heart. I thank you for accepting me for you said the gift is 'acceptable.' I thank you for this gracious meeting with yourself tonight."

Upon rising the next morning I said to my wife, "This will be a wonderful day. Last evening I received the Holy Spirit into my life as my Lord and gave Him my body to use for His glory and for the honor of the Lord Jesus. I know He will do it and He will use me without a doubt." She replied, "If anything unusual happens today, call me on the phone. I will be anxious to know." About eleven o'clock I had the joy of phoning home that the Spirit had spoken through my lips to the hearts of two young women, sisters, who had entered my office on business. Both of them trusted the Savior. This was the beginning of new days of victory, blessing, and fruitfulness which have continued since that time. I ceased to neglect and ignore this gracious Person who had come to live with me. Now He was free to use me in His service for the glory of the Lord Jesus.

Your days, too, will be transformed and your life made fruitful if you will give to the Holy Spirit the place He should have in your life.[1]

Friendship with the Spirit is the revival relationship. Will you enter into the reality of your privileged partnership? This is the need of the hour individually. But it is also the need of the hour corporately.

Pastor Ron Vanderhart, a pastor friend of mine who had invited our ministry to hold a week of revival meetings in his church in August of 2003, told me soon after my wife and son and I arrived at his church that perhaps fifteen people in his congregation had "a burning heart." He said, "God is doing something!" About a year or so earlier, the church had been going through some severe trials. At that time, Pastor Vanderhart's son, Scott, who was assistant pastor of the church, had read A. W. Tozer's book *The Pursuit of God.* A spark was ignited! As the pastor and others read the book too, soon there was a "fellowship of the burning heart." They began to meet on Saturday mornings and desperately to cry out to God for revival. One man in particular became a real intercessor.

One year later we arrived for a weeklong meeting. I had no idea of the depth at which God was already working. I would simply have the opportunity to observe a true work of God. When the pastor told me of those with "a burning heart," I began to sense that God really was doing something. By the end of the Sunday services, I had spotted many who were in this group, for their faces radiated with the burning desire for God in their hearts.

By Tuesday the truths of a clean heart and the reality of the Spirit-filled life began to take hold in some lives as the Spirit brought truth home to ready hearts. On Wednesday evening, just before the service started, the man who had become a serious intercessor in the church told me with quiet confidence that God was going to do something special that night. I preached on partnership with the Holy Spirit. After a precious service in which many responded to truth, it was announced that those who were able and so desired could reconvene in fifteen minutes for an after-meeting. I'll let excerpts from my journal tell the story:

> I publicly turned the meeting over to the Holy Spirit, encouraging each one to pray, sing, or testify only as the Spirit guided. After opening in prayer, the pastor prayed a sweet confession regarding neglecting the Holy Spirit. He was manifestly moved. Soon, his sons prayed honest,

transparent, earnest prayers. . . . There followed confession after confession with a broken spirit. Songs interspersed the praying. After a time of real cleansing, there was prayer for lost loved ones. One man prayed with real brokenness regarding the state of his children. Another lady wept and prayed over her grandchildren. Truly, God had manifested His presence! The meeting lasted for one hour and forty-five minutes.

Thursday . . . we met again for an after-meeting. The first 20–30 minutes seemed hard. Several even mentioned it in their prayers. I sensed an attack from the evil one. So I explained the basics of spiritual warfare. I urged that each one ask God to search them and deal with any sin God brought to light, but that if nothing came to light, to recognize a direct attack from the powers of darkness and to plead the blood and promises of Christ's victory over Satan at the cross. The Lord . . . prompted me to lead in singing "There Is Power in the Blood." . . . The next hour was one of the most glorious hours I, perhaps, have ever witnessed. "Where the Spirit of the Lord is; there is liberty." O what liberty! It was an hour of some of the sweetest, deepest, most earnest confessions and honesty before the Lord who knows all. God had come down. Also, there was both soul searching and glorious singing. Again, the praying turned toward a passion for the lost. The meeting lasted for over two hours and ended sometime after 11:00 p.m. On Friday . . . we definitely had increased in those who came. Again God met with us for over two hours! Many confessed failure in the gospel. We finished again around 11:00 p.m.

Nine months later the assistant pastor, Scott, told me, "There is no question. A group of people have been definitely changed!" This was God-sent revival. Nearly every time I have since spoken with Pastor Vanderhart, he has told me that the effects of the revival have continued. Friendship with the Spirit is real!

The following week, after the revival, a few of these transformed folks came to my next meeting at another church nearby. I asked several of them to give a testimony. Scott testified that ten minutes of prayer used to seem like two hours to him but that now two hours in prayer seemed like ten minutes. He also said, "If you would have asked me a week ago what revival was, I could not have told you." Then, as a tear rolled down his cheek, he said, "Now I can tell you what revival is—it's Jesus Christ!"

Oh, that we would realize that the Spirit glorifies the Son! If we partner with the Spirit, Christ will be glorified. When we develop a vibrant friendship with the Spirit, we will be aglow with the indwelling Christ! No wonder the inspired prayer of Paul was, *"The communion of the Holy Ghost be with you all. Amen."*

Questions for Personal Reflection

1. Will you give the Holy Spirit His rightful place in your life?

2. Will you ask God to spread His reviving work to other hearts?

NOTES

Chapter 1: The Revival Spirit

1. John R. Van Gelderen, *The Wind of the Spirit in Personal and Corporate Revival* (Menomonee Falls, WI: Preach the Word Ministries, 2003), 1–2.

2. Walter Wilson, *Ye Know Him* (Grand Rapids: Zondervan, 1939), 10–11.

Chapter 2: The Divine Partner

1. Jonathan Goforth, *When the Spirit's Fire Swept Korea* (Elkhart, IN: Bethel, 1984).

2. C. H. Spurgeon, *Power for You* (New Kensington, PA: Whitaker, 1996), 10–11.

Chapter 4: The Senior Partner

1. James A. Stewart, *I Must Tell* (Asheville, NC: Revival Literature, n.d.), 86–95.

2. Ruth Stewart, *James Stewart: Missionary* (Asheville, NC: Revival Literature, 1977).

Chapter 5: The Empowering Partner

1. Samuel Chadwick, *The Way to Pentecost* (Fort Washington, PA: CLC, 2001), 7–9.

Chapter 6: A Sacred Trust

1. James A. Stewart, *Heaven's Throne Gift* (Asheville, NC: Revival Literature, 2001), 66.

2. Handley C. G. Moule, *The Holy Spirit* (Tain, Ross-shire, Scotland: Christian Focus, 1999), 8.

3. A. W. Tozer in Marilynne E. Foster, comp., *Tozer on the Holy Spirit* (Camp Hill, PA: Christian Publications, 2000), devotional entry for March 24.

Chapter 7: A Spiritual Guide

1. For a thorough treatise on discerning satanic counterfeits in the spirit realm, see *War on the Saints* by Jessie Penn-Lewis with Evan Roberts (New York: Lowe, 1973). Much of what I address in this section I learned from this helpful book.

Chapter 8: The Revival Relationship

1. Wilson, *Ye Know Him*, 10–11.

RECOMMENDED READING

Cumming, James Elder. *Through the Eternal Spirit: A Bible Study on the Holy Spirit*. Minneapolis: Bethany, 1965.

Gordon, A. J. *The Ministry of the Spirit*. Minneapolis: Bethany, 1985.

McQuilkin, Robertson. *Life in the Spirit*. Nashville: Broadman & Holman, 2000.

Moule, Handley C. G. *The Holy Spirit*. Tain, Ross-shire, Scotland: Christian Focus, 1999.

Murray, Andrew. *The Spirit of Christ*. New Kensginton, PA: Whitaker, 2010.

Paxson, Ruth. *The Work of God the Holy Spirit*. Chicago: Moody, 1958.

Stewart, James A. *Heaven's Throne Gift*. Asheville, NC: Revival Literature, 2001.

Torrey, R. A. *The Person and Work of the Holy Spirit*. New Kensington, PA: Whitaker, 1996.

Wilson, Walter. *Ye Know Him*. Grand Rapids: Zondervan, 1939.

51835744R00063

Made in the USA
Lexington, KY
06 September 2019